The Genealogy of the Soul

A Personal Guide to Family Constellation Work

Patricia Jamie Lee, M.A.

Many Kites Press
Copyright © 2011 Patricia Jamie Lee

Many Kites Press

ISBN 978-1-937238-00-1

For information on trainings or workshops
with Jamie Lee or to visit her blog,
No Ordinary Life,
visit www.jamieleeonline.com

Printed in The United States

Other Books
by Patricia Jamie Lee

Fiction

Washaka—The Bear Dreamer

Albert's Manuscript

One Drum

The Wind of a Thousand Years,
story booklet for The Bead People
International Peace Project
www.thebeadpeople.org

Nonfiction

The Lonely Place
Revisioning Adolescence and the Rite of Passage

See Me Beautiful,
Charting a path to presence and strength

Dedicated to Milt

What wind of the greater soul
Blew your sand into my crevices?
So fine a grit that all my dips and hollows
Became smooth and seamless?

What sun broke through dark
Clouds the first day we awoke
Together and knew that dusk
would never again be night?

What cool water leaked
across burn and scar and
made them invisible
once again?

What scarlet bridge formed
Across what canyon
to bring you to me?
Love, only love.

The Genealogy of the Soul
A Personal Guide to Family Constellation Work
Table of Contents

Introduction

It was spring of 1999 and my mother had died just a month earlier. I was missing her terribly and feeling unsure of what to do next. For several years my husband, Milt, and I had been producing a 52-part public radio series on Native American Music. This massive project was coming to an end, and I felt rootless and unsure of what was next for me.

Then a friend invited me to attend a demonstration of Family Constellation Work being offered by a German psychotherapist named Heinz Stark. I had no idea what it was or why I should go, but Peg urged me on, and I decided to go. Although earlier in my life I'd been an NLP trainer and coach, I'd long since abandoned the therapy or self-help world. I had no intention of returning to that work.

That evening we drove twenty minutes out into the beautiful Black Hills and pulled up in front of a pretty ranch house nested in a high meadow. The spacious living room was full of the curious and slightly nervous group who had gathered there. Many of them I recognized from local seeking community.

When Heinz Stark began describing the work, I realized that we were going to do something resembling psychodrama or a Satir-like family reconstruction. Heinz invited the first person to cross the room and sit in the empty chair beside him. I leaned over to Peg and jokingly said, "Watch, I always get chosen to be the mother in these things."

Heinz scolded us for laughing and said that this field of energy must be carefully maintained. He explained that the constellation was a tool designed to show us our right place within the family of origin. He began a short interview with the client and instructed her to choose one representative from the group to stand in for her mother, another for her father, and one for herself—the client asked me to be her mother.

The woman quietly centered herself and then moved each of us into a position that only she could sense. I stood in what Heinz had called *the knowing field* as the client's mother. What happened next I still can't coherently explain. Suddenly I was flooded with thoughts, sensations, and movements that had nothing to do with my previous state of only seconds before. The sensations were, quite literally, not mine. At one point Heinz instructed the woman to choose a representative for her son. The woman moved the representative right next to me, our shoulders touching, and I felt a sudden jolt of heat. Heinz began to work with the constellation doing subtle movements and having us repeat sentences.

The process looked so simple, yet the energy grew as the constellation moved toward resolution. I was intrigued.

The most memorable constellation that night was that of a woman from a typical South Dakota ranching family. The "issue" was that she and her two sons couldn't seem to hang on to money or material goods. As the constellation unfolded, Heinz traced the family back to the woman's grandfather who had amassed large tracts of land during the Depression. It was clear that this grandfather had taken advantage of the economic suffering of others by buying out his neighbors and gaining from their loss. In other words the wealth he had amassed was based on an injustice to others. From this perspective, the constellation revealed that the great-grandsons unconsciously atoned for this injustice by not holding on to the family land or their own wealth. It also revealed that the young men were not entitled to atone for the actions of their grandfather.

The depth and authenticity of this work moved me deeply. I, like many others who take a first look, was skeptical and doubtful that a grandfather's actions could wreak such havoc on later generations. It seemed almost unbelievable.

I left that demonstration full of questions. Could this energetic and intricate linking up of loyalty through the generations of a family be true? Are we really so tied to those who came before? And what would that mean about our culture? We Americans pride ourselves on our independence, yet the scene that unfolded that night was one of hidden and powerful *interdependencies*.

By the time I went to bed that night, I knew with complete and utter certainty that my working life was about to shift again and that all my previous work experiences had been to prepare me to do this work.

In the days to follow, many of the things Heinz said that night echoed through my mind. I realized that this was not just a form of therapy but a way of looking at our primary relationships. There really is a certain *right order* within families and also within our personal and business relationships. I started reading the work of the founder of this work, Bert Hellinger, and tried putting some of the things Heinz had said into practice.

For example, I had asked Heinz what to about my ex-husband who was often gone for months at a time on his construction jobs. What about our children? I'm sure Heinz detected my resentment and anger about this issue.

He said divorced parents have to let go of their anger. "Honor the presence of the father in the son" were his exact words to me. I contemplated those words and realized that I had subtle and almost sneaky ways of keeping my children from fully accepting their father. The problem was in me—not him.

After seeing the constellation work, I decided to try and support any movement my children made toward their father. The first test of my resolve came within a week. I was out of town and had an e-mail from my then fifteen-year-old son, Thomas. He wrote, "Would it be okay with you if I worked with Dad on a job this summer?"

Summer was normally my time with the children, but Heinz had stressed how important it was for children to make a movement away from the mother and toward the father—especially in adolescence. I could hear the real question behind Thomas' email. "Is it okay with you if I go to my father?"

I wrote back instantly and gave him my full approval. I also told him a story about how funny and smart his father was—and how much he was like his father.

I nearly laughed aloud when he wrote back and asked, "Would it be okay with you if I send your email to Dad?" Tom wanted to be sure that his father knew I approved.

The release was immediate. Tom was suddenly free to go to his dad and a hidden tension—the energy of a soul whose loyalty was split between separated parents—evaporated.

This, as we'll explore in greater depth, is a critical movement—especially for divorced or separated couples with children. We need to honor the other parent in our children in order for them to be free to love us both.

Other events confirmed the power of this work. After the demonstration night, Heinz was doing a workshop, and since we didn't have funds for both of us to go, my husband, Milt, went. He was adopted and had multiple issues related to adoption. We decided he would get the greater benefit by attending.

After the workshop he came home and decided to try finding a daughter who had been adopted almost thirty years earlier. He'd not known of her existence until the adoption was already completed. Three days later he found her on the Internet, and within three weeks of exchanges with a "missing persons coordinator" we had a phone call from Susan. He has since spent several extended visits with his daughter and her children and a rich, new dimension has been added to his life.

By now, I was stunned by my meager experience with this work. In a few short months, my son had found his way to his father, and my husband had found a lost daughter.

I began exploring my own patterns of depression and family connection. My first constellation with Heinz later that fall took about five minutes. I mentioned that my mother had died recently and that my father was deceased. Heinz simply chose two representatives, one for my mother and one for my father. When I stood up in that pesky "knowing field" I simply burst into tears and ran into the arms of my "parents" to feel their love surround me for just one more moment. It was sweet and painful and powerful. Later—I think I was feeling like I hadn't gotten my money's worth—I mentioned to Heinz that my constellation was *pretty small*. He smiled at me and said mysteriously, "There are no small constellations."

And it's true. Over ten years later, I am still surrounded by the love of my deceased parents whenever I hold that image.

Finally, I approached Heinz Stark and asked, "What can I do to help? I want to learn this work." Family Constellation

Work was still brand new in America although it was growing rapidly in Germany and Europe. There were no formal U.S. training programs, so I followed Heinz Stark through a year of intense workshops acting as both his student and his coordinator.

After training with Heinz I began offering first a study group, then a training/practice group, and eventually I gained enough confidence to actually do workshops. The original draft of this book came about because I wanted a way for my workshop attendees to be able to explore the concepts of the constellation on their own with simple concepts and practical exercises. Since then, I've revised it to include people who have not attended a workshop but are curious about the work. I hope this guide will point a direction for you to strengthen your stand in life within your existing systems.

Chapter 1 offers an introduction to Family or Systemic Constellation Work as both a form of therapy and a way of thinking about relationships. Then it separates into exploring the specific topics or relationships. I've included exercises to help you personalize the concepts. After reading the orientation, browse the book by topic or explore it in whatever way suits you.

There are occasional references to earlier decades of my life. In the eighties I worked with individuals using a technology called Neurolinguistic Programming or NLP. Later I spent ten years writing and producing public radio documentaries with my husband, Milt Lee. Then I returned to the human development path with this work.. Writing stories, novels, and books has been a common thread throughout all the working decades of my life.

The names and examples here have been scrambled to protect the privacy of those who have trusted me or others to enter their family systems. I will mix up the gender by using "he" or "she" rather than the annoying repetition of "he or she". What is presented here is based on my own experience as a facilitator and a student of the work of Bert Hellinger. Any lack of clarity belongs with me. I would also like to thank Heinz Stark and Bert Hellinger and the other German facilitators who traveled such a distance to bring this work to us Americans.

Chapter One
An Orientation to
Family Constellation Work

The Origins of Constellation Work

In his earlier years, Bert Hellinger was a Catholic Priest working with the Zulu people in Africa as an educational administrator. He became very involved with both the people and the culture. One of the stories he told was about a seminar he attended on group dynamics. He said that at some point during the training the facilitator asked them what they cared more about—principles or people? Hellinger said that that question stuck in his mind. He went home that night and could hardly sleep because he kept asking himself whether he cared more about principles—or people. In the end, he decided that he cared more about people. He began to study family dynamics and systems work in greater depth and even ended up leaving the priesthood to pursue this new passion fully.

Over the years of working with individuals and families he began to notice deep loyalties that seemed to exist within families no matter what external circumstances existed. Such loyalties often made no logical sense but seemed to exist anyway. Much of his work was happening in post WWII Germany where many families had been torn apart by the war.

What Hellinger observed, and what the tribal elders in clan systems around the world have known instinctively, is that life flows down through the generations of a family from the oldest to the youngest. Two separate families are joined each time a child is born and the new life flows forward to the future. This blood tie is strong and resilient and loyal. Hellinger thought of these ties to our lineage as the natural law or order of families. The more he worked with families, the more he realized that when the "order" is observed in a good way, life goes on in a good way. When something happens to disrupt this natural order, life begins to move toward disorder. This became the basis of Family Constellation Work.

The Goal of Constellation Work

With a word like "constellation," one thinks of stars arranging themselves into patterns in the distant skies—but this constellation takes place in the inner space of the family system, one member placed in relationship to another. Constellation work—or what we might call *family soul work*—traces the soul through the ancestral lineage of the family.

The goal of constellation work is two-fold and sometimes this appears to be at cross purposes. The first goal is to help us to gain personal strength by connecting to our own lineage. The second goal is to make sure we have *separated* from our lineage and are free to begin our own new system. If we are caught up in the fate of our parents or ancestors, we cannot freely move ahead into our own future. This is called an entanglement. An entanglement binds up our personal energy and keeps us stuck. The Constellation is a tool to reveal this entanglement and to gain release and freedom from whatever that is. We'll be exploring dozens of possible entanglements as we move through the topics of the book.

To be a strong adult who can fulfill the many roles required of us as children, partners, parents, coworkers and grand-parents, we need all of our energy. If we are caught in past patterns, we remain stuck in childlike patterns and unable to use our life energy. Hellinger speaks eloquently of the difference between the "blind love of a child" and what he calls "the enlightened love of an adult." As adults, we are at last able to see that our parents were also children and, in recognizing that, fully take our place as adults.

According to Hellinger, we often maintain our childlike ways out of loyalty and love to the parents and the family. Again, paradoxically, we seek both a stronger connection to our lineage—and the freedom to separate and go forward. When we are entangled with earlier events or family members, we are not free to do either in a good way.

The constellation gives us a tool for making these entanglements visible, but we have to realize that these hidden loyalties flowing deep within the families can be obscured and difficult to resolve. We also have to realize that the constellation is not a specific formula that *cures* issues. It's a fluid, organic process that we must approach humbly and with openness.

For instance, in the constellation I described earlier where the grandfather had amassed land and wealth on the back of his neighbors, the "solution" was for the grandsons to return that burden of guilt to the grandfather—and to let him carry the consequences. As younger members of a system, the grandsons were not entitled to "atone" for what grandfather had done. In handing back the burden of guilt, the grandsons could now be free to build their own prosperity. This will become more clear as we move through the concepts of the work.

The Hidden Orders of Love

In the greater soul of the family, there is a loving glue that binds one generation to another, that crosses known boundaries of time and space, and even operates in the gray zone between life and death. The constellation process gives us visible access to that flow of love and loyalty within the family. We can see both its purity, and the ways in which it obstructs our movements.

When we are entangled or have taken on the pain, guilt, or sadness of someone within our system, we generally can't see that we have done so. The entanglement is hidden from view, operating outside conscious awareness. We are aware that life is not going smoothly—but we have no idea why. We seek outside answers or begin to berate ourselves for not being motivated enough—or smart enough—to get it right. An incredible amount of energy is expended trying to heal what we *think* is the problem while the true source remains obscured.

Essentially, we all carry a membership card for our own family of origin. This membership connects us energetically to the other members of our system. Time and space are not factors. We can sever all connections and move three thousand miles away and discover, for all our grand efforts, that we are as tightly linked as ever. Like a Chinese finger cuff made of paper—the harder we pull, the tighter the lock. Not even death can interfere with these mysterious links. Each member of a system has a singular place and that place must be held or the flow of love becomes disordered.

Bert Hellinger calls the rules of belonging within our family system, "The Hidden Orders of Love." These hidden orders exist outside of what social conscience might call right or wrong, good or bad and continue to operate even when we pretend they don't. They simply are—like the laws of nature, like water that must flow downhill, or winter that must come at a certain time. We all own a particular place in our family. To our parents, we will always be a child. To our children, we will always be a parent. The orders are fixed and immutable no matter the many ways human beings will mess with them.

Discovering what Hellinger termed, "the hidden orders of love" is more than simply generational order or a therapeutic tool. These natural orders are, in fact, a philosophical orientation toward life itself. In shorthand form, the orders of love are:

- All who have a place in a system must be included and their place held;
- A younger member of the system is not entitled to interfere with the fate of an older member;
- One generation passes the life on to the next and, like the natural laws of gravity, the flow is always toward the future;
- We must all carry the consequences of our own actions;
- There is a larger force at work to which we must all submit.

What appears so simple in a bulleted list like this becomes much more complex in the daily practice of living. Most of us stumble along without realizing that we may be coming into conflict within our familial or ancestral systems. Additionally, larger social or cultural systems also have their own "hidden orders" for membership and belonging, but they tend to be less binding than the loyalty ties to the family. Religions, nations, even small community groups all evolve and form their own systems. We will also take a look at these in later chapters. These systems are complex.

For example, I worked with a mother who said her sixteen-year-old daughter was depressed and acting out—making poor decisions. She was being sent to a wellness program to *get it fixed*. As we worked on the daughter, I found out Mom had been divorced twice, her mother had been divorced twice, the girl's father had experienced the suicide of a little brother. In this too-typical picture, the young girl was clearly acting as the little pack mule for the family, taking on and carrying the stuff of the family on her tender shoulders. Sadly, she was also being asked to do the penance and serve the sentence for what she had not caused and could not cure.

As you read the following pages, do so with openness and a receptive mind. Set aside for a moment what you think you know about human relationships and families. Notice not what your mind says but what your heart or soul says. Remember that the cord that binds is always love and deep loyalty—even in the face of ugliness or adversity.

There will be those among you that resist some of the ideas presented here. I have heard many of your concerns in my talks and workshops and ask only that you consider for a moment the loving logic behind this philosophical view of how a family works.

The examples provided here are intended to be descriptive—not prescriptive. Constellation work is a specific tool for a specific purpose. It is not a quick fix for missing life strategies. Most of the time, we are unaffected by the actions of those who came before, and we will be misled if we begin arbitrarily drawing lines of connection between family members and events in our own lives. We end up creating another useless story to explain why life does not go well. It is not our goal to uncover secrets or to place blame but to discover both the source and the solution to our current situation. We go to our family system with a humble heart—looking for answers.

Our goal is to discover if we are carrying something that doesn't belong to us. What is mine, I am held accountable for; what belongs to another, I give back to them; and what operates in the larger, unknown forces of the world, I can only bow to and hope one day to understand its deeper meaning.

What a Constellation Looks Like

Here is an example of a constellation. A woman, I will call her Bertie, comes to the group and expresses that she has been sad and depressed for most of her life. She is educated, has a solid marriage, three children, and feels she has no real reason to feel sad. Traditional therapies and self-help have had little or no effect.

A constellation always begins with a fact-finding mission. We ignore old narratives and go for actual events within the family. In Bertie's case her mom and dad are still alive and still married. She is the oldest of four children and there are no significant events such as war, immigration, trauma, etc. to her knowledge. I ask about any known missing family members, and she suddenly recalls that Mom did have a stillborn child but not much was ever said about how the child died. It simply isn't talked about. I instruct her to choose representatives for herself, Mom, Dad, and the stillborn child and to set them up in a constellation.

Setting up a family constellation is deceptively simple. The client chooses representatives from the available group members to stand in for each of the selected members, including a representative for herself. Once the representatives are selected, the client places her hands on each one's shoulders, and then intuitively moves the representatives into the circle. When the representatives have been placed, the client sits and watches as the constellation unfolds. The facilitator counsels representatives that their only job is to report—not to role-play or act.

Setting up a constellation brings the hidden patterns into the visible field. As the representatives stand where they have been placed, they experience the sensations and qualities of the person they represent—a mysterious process we will discuss in a later chapter. The facilitator then enters the field, first taking stock of the initial picture and noting the location of each representative such as who is isolated, who is center, who is looking away or at each other. This early assessment by the facilitator is a combination of intuition, training, knowledge, and experience. What is this picture saying? Each representative is asked to report any information such as physical sensations, movements, or thoughts that occur to them.

In this particular constellation, we notice initially that all members look away from each other, and the client's representative stands apart from the rest. Dad reports numbness. Mom reports cold hands and a pain in her abdomen with attending sadness. The deceased stillborn child reports feeling anxious and afraid and the client's representative simply feels cut off from life and from the others.

In the past, Virginia Satir and other family systems therapists have used representatives, circles on a page, or placement of objects to create a similar picture of the family system, but Hellinger took a pioneering step by accepting the revealed picture as a *living communication* from the system itself. Then he sought to restore order where disorder had prevailed.

With Bertie, I begin a series of trial and error movements relying strongly on the reports of the representatives to discover and restore the right order in this system. I have both Mom and Dad face the stillborn child and test a series of sentences spoken to the child. Mom says, "I couldn't look at you. My pain was too great." And then, "Now I dare to look at you and realize that in this pain is my love for you."

The facilitator is not *operating on* but *operating within* the system. I follow the natural flow. If I give a representative a sentence to say, but she says, "No, that doesn't feel right," I this response and seek the truer statement.

Bertie's constellation unfolds in trial and error stages as we discover the right movements for all the representatives. The representative for the stillborn child is placed with the siblings and the parents feel deeply relieved. Then I have Bertie "meet" her sister. Here also are a series of trial and error movements and statements such as, "It's good to see you, dear sister. I miss you." This brings the final release and the natural order is restored.

The constellation moves from the first picture into a series of trial movements as we find and restore the natural order. Generally, it ends when all the representatives feel good again. In Bertie's case, the pain of losing the child caused the family to try to forget the pain. In the forgetting, the unborn child lost her place. As we have seen, often another sibling will take on the burden of that loss and feel sad or "empty."

At this point, Bertie is encouraged to take the new picture fully into her soul and to allow it to begin further movements toward resolution.

This highly simplified example is just one of the many possible configurations a constellation can reveal. Unlike many therapeutic models, this one requires that the facilitator take an almost Zen-like approach. He or she must be loose and willing to move with whatever is presented within the field holding only a general framework of the hidden orders of love, the known facts of the family, and the reports of the representatives.

Little attention is given to the family "story" as the client has learned to interpret it. Many of us have spent a lifetime trying to explain why we feel bad or why things aren't going well. These stories or family scripts offer little in the way of understanding these hidden dynamics. The constellation generally reveals ties and connections we had not formerly even considered. The facilitator is willing to be curious, surprised, and flexible. A good facilitator is also one who has probed his or her own family system thoroughly to prevent blind spots and directions coming from his or her own soul.

I remember, when my training group first began, many of us would sit through constellations in tears or vibrating with some issue that resonated with our own. We had to clear this out before we could begin to work.

Every constellation is different in the picture that it presents. People have used it to resolve issues with a marriage, a relationship with a child or a parent, and to look into a health issue such as depression, mental illness or physical illness. The constellation process is even currently being used to look into the less powerful relationships within organizations and businesses or cultures which will be discussed in a later chapter. However, each constellation begins with a sincere question and a desire for some shift in our current reality.

In some cases, a person can be severely disturbed with multiple entanglements. I think this plays a stronger role in "mental illness" than we have previously considered. Awhile back I got into reading true crime stories such as Ann Rule. I was amazed at how often severe criminal acts were preceded by multiple and confusing issues within the family. The father is absent, the child is raised as another person's child, the mother's father committed suicide, and on and on. In one story, a child was named Colette, but the story revealed that she was the fifth Collette to be born in the family. The first four died at birth or before but were still given the name "Collette." The writers of these true crime stories have probably not studied constellation work but these stories underscore the importance of Hellinger's "hidden orders." This work touches something true and sure inside of us when we witness it.

How Does the Constellation Work?

In an age where the drug companies and the medical model increasingly blame our "disorders" on biology, DNA or neurology, I am increasingly intrigued by this idea of a holistic web of energetic connection. One day science may be able to understand these energy fields better. Personally, I like the term, "the family soul." There is much that the shamans and yogis have understood about the universe that science has not yet reached.

The constellation demonstrates the possibility of a wider connectedness than we previously may have considered. Are we really tied into the complex web of our ancestral line? Can the earlier actions of others affect us in this generation? Just as Carl Jung tentatively introduced his idea of the collective unconscious, so Hellinger gives us the phenomenological tool of the constellation as a way of connecting energetically with our ancestral line. We can't necessarily understand these hidden forces at work, but we can use them.

To see this played out within the constellation can be stunning. Representatives act like small antennae able to pick up on accurate and powerful information belonging to another. Again and again my clients report that the mannerisms, expressions, and even exact information provided by the representatives are uncannily accurate.

In one workshop, the representative for a client's mother began limping on her right leg. The client reported that the mother had recently crushed her knee in a motorcycle accident. In another case the representative for the client's father got very dizzy and disoriented, and the client reported that her father died of Parkinson's disease. The representatives did not have these details until after they experienced it. This occurs so frequently that those of us working within this "knowing field" trust that the reports of representatives are accurate and useful.

For many of us the logical mind needs an explanation and casts about trying to understand the phenomenon. We talk of morphogenic fields, physics, the spiritual web of connection,

15

shamanic forces; we make up all manner of ways to explain phenomenological experience.

Personally, I think that just like we have a *genetic* blueprint in the physical body—we also have an *energetic* blueprint of our larger system. This is the substance of the family constellation. We are connected both physically and spiritually to the larger system of our family. Another way to consider it is that setting up a constellation creates a kind of hologram for the client—through them, we can see the whole.

For several years I worked with a group on the Pine Ridge Reservation under the guidance of a medicine man. Within the Lakota culture, the involvement of spirits and the ancestors is never taken lightly. Before I could begin doing constellation work with this group, I had to agree to go into the *Inipi* (sweat lodge) so the medicine man could ask the spirits permission. As a white woman, I had never been in a sweat lodge.

Although I am married to a tribal member and have spent my life around native people, I felt awkward and unsure about entering the *Inipi* ceremony. It is not my culture. I was also a bit worried about the heat—I have a touch of claustrophobia. I asked the wife of the medicine man who is also a friend if there was anything I should know—protocols and parameters. She eased my fears instantly. "Just think of the steam as the breath of the grandfathers and ask for their help." This was so consistent with my experience with this work that I went in and each blast of steam brought me a greater connection instead of discomfort.

The spirits agreed that this work was needed for their people. However, the spirits also said that it was important to acknowledge the true source of the help we received. Following each constellation session, we were to again enter the *Inipi* and ask to be cleansed—and to release the ancestors back to the spirit world.

For the next year I worked monthly with their group. For the traditional Lakota, the distance between the realms of the living and the realms of the dead is not so vast. Before each constellation session, we prayed and smudged with sage or cedar, praying to the ancestors for their help. I found it wonderful to work within a culture that did not question the

16

involvement of the other realms. It helped me come to terms with my own beliefs about why the constellation works.

Regardless of how we explain or understand the information gleaned by the representatives in a constellation, my experience tells me that we can trust what it provides when we approach the work in a spiritual and highly respectful way. When we do so, help comes to guide us toward a solution and the right order.

Whether we choose physics or a shamanic explanation for the help that arrives in the constellation, it is clear to me that without this deep respect the constellation this would become simply one more therapeutic method. Family Constellation Work is not an A to B to C method, but an intuitive process that unfolds when the group forms.

Facilitating Constellation Work

To be effective working within this energetic field, a practitioner must have the right stuff. First, we need to resolve our own entanglements and issues to avoid blind spots. Secondly, we must let go of all previous belief systems about what is right and wrong about incest, death, abortion, murder, and so called good or bad parents. In the larger soul of the family, there are only actions, consequences of those actions, and the glue that binds the whole. This glue is love and loyalty, even when it appears to be something quite different. We approach the field with an attitude of acceptance and non-judgment. This is not an easy state to achieve. Finally, we need training to recognize the "hidden orders" within families that mysteriously become visible within the field of the constellation.

Constellation work is not a set of ritual movements that can be performed in a perfunctory fashion while looking at a manual in your right hand. During one of my workshops an interested participant sat and wrote down all of my ritual sentences as if those sentences contained the heart of the work.

In an early workshop on the Pine Ridge Reservation in South Dakota, a Lakota man explained that in their culture working with the ancestors requires that we become a "hollow bone." In other words, we set aside all knowledge and thought and become a pipe through which the information coming from a larger source can flow. The hollow bone is a good description of the state of an effective facilitator—and of the whole group that comes together to support the constellation work. Personal ego, the mind, thoughts, concepts, and ideas have little value within this knowing field.

We can't learn all the complexities of this work until we actually enter the field as a practitioner. To learn it, we must do it—and we must humbly take the tools and integrate them into who we are and not simply become little clones of our trainer. I expect to always be a student of this work and never a master. Within the mysterious workings of the constellation tool, I recognize that to know is to know that you don't know. We take a humble stance and go forward.

However, you don't have to become a facilitator to begin integrating these principles into your life. Begin with this manual and your own family of origin. Be willing to set aside common family stories or the many reasons you have told yourself that life is not going so well. We often assume that one or the other parent wasn't supportive enough, and begin to hang our own failures on this too-familiar hook. Unfortunately, many therapies help us to choose this easy out. It takes courage and strength to begin setting aside common stories and to look deeply into the true origins of our family with adult eyes. Be open learners, ready to explore and experiment in a respectful way.

A word of caution. If you are seeking an opportunity to look at your own family by doing a constellation, choose a facilitator carefully. Besides checking on training and level of experience, perhaps the most important indicator is to look directly at the person. Does he or she have a good, full life? Is she strong? Is he succeeding at what he wants to do? These simple questions can direct you toward a good facilitator or teacher of this work. This same rule applies to choosing a therapist or coach for any inner work. Choose someone who has a life that you admire, qualities you would like to model, and a solid strength in the world. The yellow pages or a glitzy brochure won't tell you anything.

A final note about constellation work; doing a formal constellation with a trained facilitator is intended to reveal hidden entanglements with your relationship systems. It is not a cure all to life's daily problems but a specific tool for a specific purpose.

Having said this, there is a wonderful body of knowledge and understanding within constellation work that we can use to explore our place in the world and our relationships. We can use a simple process of constellating small objects in order to see a basic dynamic operating within a relationship. Gaining an understanding of the basic premises of constellation work and how to use them is the focus of this book. Personally, I can hardly talk without beginning to rearrange small coffee creamers or glasses on a restaurant table.

Recently I had a call from my sister who was having supper with a friend of hers on the East Coast. They'd been talking about constellation work, and my sister was using sugar packets to show her friend how it works. The woman had a little brother who had died very early and they called me "mid-constellation."

My sister asked, "Does she have to put the brother in his place with his siblings? My friend doesn't want to. She says they were always angry with this little brother for dying early and upsetting Mom and Dad."

I told her, "Yes—give the little brother his proper place."

So, a thousand miles away, two women were doing constellation work with sugar packets. Later my sister said that as soon as her friend put the little brother in his right place a deep, relieving wave of sadness came over her. Afterwards, the woman carried the little packet around for days trying to decide what to do with it.

Finally, during a visit to her mom, she took the small sugar packet and dumped it into her mother's sugar bowl. She decided to leave the small, sweet package with her mother—where it belonged. She called my sister several weeks later to say how incredible she felt—free and light, released from some burden she had long carried. She said the table-top constellation was worth thousands of dollars of therapy. This is the potential benefit of constellation work.

So, be cautious but be curious. Simple, little constellations like the one above can yield great results. It is, of course, best to deal with serious issues with a trained facilitator, but the first part of a constellation, getting the visible picture of hidden dynamics, can be done in small ways.

The constellation is essentially a group process. There is no real substitute for the full process, but throughout this handbook there will be opportunities for you to do a number of exercises that, though they may be limited, can nevertheless be useful in helping you to see more of your system. At the end of each topic from here on there will be sections on "Things to Consider" and then actual exercises that invite you to write or to do small constellation movements either alone or with just another person or two. There will also be many trial ritual sentences included in the exercise section for each topic. As in a full constellation, trust your own soul to know which sentences have energy—and which ones are inert and have no effect.

To do these exercises, you may want to gather a few small objects to work with. I have used small stones, little wooden pegs, seashells, water glasses on a kitchen table—or sugar packets. Choose things that can indicate a forward direction— like the face of a person. It can be important to know which direction a "representative" is facing. When a representative is turned away from other family members or from life itself, he is often placed looking outside of the circle. You may also use small pillows, shoes, or other objects that allow you to work within the open space of your living room or an office. You may want to try several things and see what works for you. The exercises will direct you more specifically as we move through each topic. My experience with these small constellations is that they can often give you new information although they may not be able to lead you to full resolution of the issue the way a trained facilitator can.

Exercise 1
A Beginning Practice Exercise Using Pillows

1. Begin with this simple tuning-in exercise. Consider something that you are trying to make a future decision about, something with only two or three possible choices.

2. Choose a number of objects to represent these possible choices—pillows would work well for this. In an empty space in your house, pick up one pillow and hold it a minute and consider one of the choices.

3. Now walk quietly around the empty space and then set the pillow down wherever it feels intuitively right to put it. Pause a moment and then pick up the second pillow, consider the second choice thoughtfully, and then again move around the space until you feel an urge to set it down. If there is a third choice, do the same process.

4. Now, turn all of your attention inward to your own sensations, thoughts, and feelings. This can mean anything from a tingle in your finger tips to changes in the temperature of your body. Walk slowly and meditatively around the space where you have placed your "choices" and notice any pull toward or away from one or the other, any sensations that arise as you approach or leave one behind.

You are new to this experience, so never mind if your brain tells you that you are being silly or crazy—and be perfectly willing to let your inner self lead you to the "right" decision. Consider that some deeper part of you already knows which choice would best serve your needs right now—you are simply getting out of your own way and letting that become more visible.

Although this is a simple training exercise for understanding that everything around us has *energy*, it can be a good way to practice this process. When you have finished simply notice what this experience brought you. If you have a clear indication of the right choice, then the next step is to learn to trust this intuitive process and act on this decision. You may even say aloud to the pillow—I choose you.

Exercise 2
On Your Own With Constellation Work

On my office table I have a pretty basket full of stones, seashells, and small wooden pegs that, when arranged, look like little people. I use these objects to constellate a client's family system. While not as effective as a real constellation—the objects can't talk or feel—it can provide useful information and insight.

1. To do a tabletop constellation, clear your mind of all the other clutter of the day.

2. Create an empty space on the table.

3. Focus your energy on the relationship you are trying to see more clearly. Then, using whatever objects are handy, assign each object the name of the person or persons you want to constellate. Use something that has a front and a back so that you can see which way the small representative is facing.

4. Now place the items in relationship to one another, keeping it clear in your mind that each piece represents and following your own intuitive sense. Let your mind be free of any preformed pictures.

5. When you've completed the setup, take a look at the distance between each member of the system, the direction they are facing, and your own feelings as you touch each one. Allow yourself to take a distant stance—as if you are looking at them from afar. What do you see? Do they look at one another? Does any member look as if they are leaving the space? What feeling do you get as you look at them? You might even touch each piece again to see if any feelings or

sensations are present such as sadness or anger, a tingling sensation, or whatever comes.

6. If you get clarity about how these people are relating to one another, see if you can find the most satisfying position for each one. Move the pieces around—bring them closer or farther apart, have them face one another. Notice any words that come to your mind as you do this.

This handy tool is not meant to resolve big issues but it can be instructive and useful in bringing some dynamic more into visibility. You may use it to get clarity on relationships, decisions, and other things as we will explore later.

In the chapters that follow, we will be examining the many different relationships and combinations. Spend time with the ones most important to you.

Chapter Two
The Family of Origin

Mother and Father

Every child is linked at conception to two ancestral lines—that of the mother and the father. In a beautiful description I heard from a Lakota Healer, the tiny spirit travels from the spirit world at the moment of conception and irrevocably enters the ancestral lines of both parents. This voyage occurs both in the physical realm and in the spirit world. The sexual act, where a child can potentially be conceived, should not be taken lightly because the consequences are forever. This linking of two ancestral lines is a profound and sacred act.

In Lakota traditional thought, tribal members are taught to consider their actions in terms of how they will affect their offspring seven generations from now. The Bible says that the sins of the father will be visited on the sons. In systemic thinking, this membership into our system of origin is not revoked if the infant is stillborn, dies in the womb, or is aborted. At conception, our place is defined and secured. A life has been created and this life must be seen if order is to be maintained.

As a child of my family system, I'm forever entwined with my parents and their parents and so on. Like a grove of Aspen trees, we share a common root system. On the simplest physical level, we have no choice. On a metaphysical level, perhaps it is a larger force that determines into which family the little flickering spirit will enter. This force we can only contemplate. Our goal is to work with what can be seen on the visible level.

Within the sphere of the family, mother and father are like two separate chalices that the child can and must drink from in order to be fully able to drink of life later. Each cup, mother and father, contains a little bit different tincture. We all basically begin life in the sphere of the mother, drinking fully and taking nourishment of the female sphere. Then, in early adolescence, (if development is on course), we move away from mother and

25

spend time in the sphere of the father in order to find our life legs and gain strength and stability.

This movement is natural and necessary for both boys and girls, although each takes the offerings a little differently. For instance, the boy moves toward manhood and the girl toward womanhood, but both have a need to be seen by the father. When something prevents this movement—divorce, death, or other severe circumstances—the child is affected adversely. The child may get stuck in the female sphere, unable to gain the strength they need.

A child must drink from both cups fully. From the female sphere comes the nourishment, the ability to nourish others, and the sensitivity to see beyond the self. This is where we begin to trust that the world is a safe and nourishing place. From the sphere of the father comes strength, a sense of our own sexual identity, and the ability to take action. I say "the sphere of" because these qualities can still be present when mother or father are not. We can consider them the female and male energies. If a child is raised by grandparents or others, the dynamics remain the same. Many of my clients recall an uncle or grandparent who filled the bill when necessary.

Our culture is sometimes not supportive of the intact family. It is estimated that over 25 million children are growing up without their fathers at home. This appears often in the constellation as well. I see many people who lack father (or male) strength and energy. They have been cut off from or heard their fathers criticized by others for many years.

In 2005, Milt did a series of letters between three daughters and their father who was in prison. The girls had not seen their father in over ten years. A very generous and courageous mother made the video letter possible, and it is a beautiful testament of how important fathers are in the lives of all children. You can see the transformation on their young faces as all the anger and old stories about dad dissolve and the love is allowed to come forward. Sometimes I catch myself humming an old song and changing the words. Mothers—don't let your babies grow up to be fatherless.

In a recent workshop the participants began jokingly talking about their "daddy deficit." A daddy deficit results in not enough male energy or strength with many symptoms—lack of boundaries, unable to face conflict, depression, unresolved relationship issues, womanizing, addiction to food, alcohol, shopping, etc.

Parents are the portals through which life flows to the children. Regardless of their own burdens, if we made it into life, two people made that possible.

Things to Consider

In the constellation process, every piece of work begins with the facilitator interviewing the client for family information. Since we don't have the benefit of being face to face, you can begin by doing your own interview. Remember that all families have losses and events that disturb the natural order of things. Look at each of the following questions and consider what you know about your family. We are just taking note and not placing any meaning on your answers at this point. We will follow this with a first set up of a table-top constellation for you to see the energetic dynamics of your family.

If you were adopted or displaced from your family for some reason and cannot answer these questions for yourself, be patient and we'll explore many of the circumstances that would keep a child from his or her family. The questions are similar to what most facilitators would begin asking within the group process. If you have a small notebook, you may want to write down your answers.

Exercise 1
The Family Interview

1. Are your natural parents still together or separated?

2. If they are separated, how old were you when they parted?

3. Were either of your parents married before or involved in a significant relationship prior to each other?

4. Were there any children born to either of your parents that you know of prior to them becoming your parents or following a separation?

5. Were there any significant events that may have had an effect on your family? Consider early deaths of a parent or sibling, war or immigration, early illnesses, mental illness or substance abuse. Please consider only the known facts and not what family narratives may have developed about these events.

6. Are there any family members who have been excluded? Consider the "black sheep" or the family skeleton.

7. Were there any children born of your parents who did not survive? Were there any siblings of your parents who did not survive or died early?

8. Do your parents or any of your siblings struggle with severe anger, depression, or sexual issues that you know of?

Note: When looking into the lives of parents or ancestors, you are essentially not entitled to know their business but seek this information only as a way of helping you or your children. Be respectful if you ask parents or relatives any sensitive questions.

Exercise 2
Constellating the Family of Origin

This will be your first attempt at doing your own constellation work with your family of origin. Please understand that although there is no group or facilitator, you can use this exercise to begin to see the hidden field of energy flowing between family mem-bers. Be willing to be surprised and open to whatever first impressions you have of your small constellation. Choose a time when your house is quiet and you are feeling a nice interior energy.

1. Lay out the items you chose in the earlier exercise (small stones, shells, wooden pegs, even beads) or, if you want to use a larger space, use pillows. Make sure that you understand which side of the object is the face.

2. Clear a space on your kitchen table, a coffee table or sit on the floor—whatever pleases you. Make sure the space is not too wide open.

3. Now center your own inner energies and then choose "representatives" from your small objects or pillows. Choose one to represent your mother, one for father, and one for yourself. Don't worry about siblings yet as we will be talking about them later.

4. Now, pick up one of the objects and be sure you remember who that object represents. Place it slowly and intuitively into the space you have outlined. It is important that this movement come from your fingertips and not from some idea or image you have in your mind. Keep out all residual or old pictures relating to the family. Do the same for both your parents and yourself.

5. Now, sit back and just look at each object. Notice any impressions, sensations, thoughts, or feelings that come up. You can put your fingers or hands on each one to reconnect with the energy of that person.

Notice if any of the figures are "facing out" away from one of the others or if one object seems distant or separated from the others. This is all just taking in the visible picture of the normally invisible energy dynamics of your family.

6. If you like journaling, you might want to take your notebook, write the date, and then record your impressions. Sometimes writing helps us deepen the impressions.

There is nothing that you need to *do* here except notice your impression of how your family picture looks. You may also have an intuitive experience about the small knowing field itself, for instance sometimes sadness, fear, or anger can be floating around the system even if you are not sure who it belongs to. If you had a strong impression such as this, you might choose an object to represent that general sensation and then move it around the field, and see if you get a further impression about whether that little feeling package belongs to mother, father, yourself, or something or someone not represented. You cannot do this wrong. Trust your impressions.

Exercise 3
Ritual Honoring Movements

Before you dismantle your constellation, try the following ritual movement and sentences. If it does not feel comfortable to you, you can simply stop and put the pieces back into a bowl or box for later and end the constellation. If it feels right, continue. You will know and should trust your inner self.

1. Place the parents side by side. If they have divorced or separated, you can leave a little space between them. Place the man on your left and the woman on your right. Now take the representative for yourself and place it before the parents and then repeat the following sentences aloud. Be sure to notice any inner responses you may have to the sentences.

"You are my parents and I am your child."
"I received my life from the both of you
and it is a gift I can never repay."
"Dear Mother, thank you."
"Dear Father, thank you."

If you have children, you may also include the following sentence.

"Because of both of you, I have children of
my own and life goes forward."

When you have finished, you may break up the field of the constellation by simply picking up the pieces and dismantling the arrangement. Although the constellation itself is completed, it often happens that the energy continues to flow on, and you may have additional thoughts and feelings later on. You can continue to note these in your journal but gather impressions the way you would gather flowers—without judgment or harshness. Be gentle with all that comes up for you. We have many more miles to travel.

31

Early Interruptions in the Natural Flow

At times serious events at the moment of birth or early trauma can have later consequences in our ability to enjoy life fully. The brief description below is not a diagnosis, but simply another direction to look when life is not going smoothly. The interference in the birth process is fate (not considered systemic) and can have a powerful effect on us.

When circumstances occur that prevent the newborn infant from bonding fully and immediately with the mother an interruption happens. Hellinger describes this as an "interruption of the reaching out movement." A heavily-drugged birthing mom, cesarean birth, critical illness of mom or infant, or even later illnesses that cause a separation can all influence our ability to complete the reaching out movement.

The signs of this interrupted movement are a cycling toward and away from what we most want. For example, a person sets out to get a college degree, completes several years, and then quits. A few years later, he again starts college—only to quit. Or a woman engages in a loving relationship but when it comes time to commit, she leaves. We move toward something—and then back away. I've often heard this pattern called "fear of success." Hellinger calls this interruption of the reaching out movement, "the cause of all neurosis."

At the moment of birth, there are many biological systems in the infant that are turning on--organ functions, brain functions, muscle functions, and the like. These switches are turned on by the birth process itself and the subsequent stroking, nursing, bonding with the mother. One research project indicated that animals lick their infants not to clean them but to stimulate essential reticulating brain processes necessary for later life. The bonding of human infant to mother is the same. It is not just psychological—but biological. An early interruption interferes with this essential function and with the later reaching out movement.

Imagine the small arms of a babe reaching out toward Mommy or Daddy with total trust and need only to have the movement cut off suddenly. When this happens the child learns to distrust, fearing that any reaching out movement will only lead to disappointment.

As I work more and more with constellation clients, I can almost see an early interruption in the physiology of the person. She has a pinched, squinted look, an eyes-not-quite-open-on-the-world-look. There is also often a thin, almost skeletal appearance that indicates an inability to "take in" nourishment and other things necessary for life.

In constellation work, when the client has had such an interruption, it's possible for the facilitator to act as the mother—or to select a representative for mother—and to allow the child to reenact the movement and complete it. This takes many forms in the group process. I've seen tremendous benefit for those who allow themselves to fully feel the movement and to go with the reaching out, but it should be done only with a trained facilitator.

I was once describing constellation work to several of my fellow graduate students in an empty dining room in a monastery in St. Paul, Minnesota. After several minutes of talking one of the women said, "Can't we just see a small demonstration?" I had Susan set up Janet as her mother. It was clear even from our small constellation that the mother was heavily-burdened and sad. Susan completed a movement of giving back to the mother what belonged to her. It was a very touching and rich moment, but after we were done Janet said suddenly, "I don't feel very well, this is like, ah, making me so sad . . . ."

With her permission, I sat across from her and told her to imagine me as her mother. I had her breathe deeply into the sadness and need she felt and then, when it was right, to say, "Mom, please, I need you."

She made a beautiful movement toward her mother with her arms coming up slowly and fully, reaching at last what she has wanted for so long. It was powerful. Janet was shocked at how emotional she became—and how clear she felt afterwards. I remembered hearing her speak earlier about how unsure she felt about doing this graduate program. I suspect that she'd drawn near and pulled away from many things in her life.

In another constellation workshop, a woman reported that her mother nearly died from a severe case of toxemia when she was born. Jane, now in her adult life, had very severe allergies and was always monitoring what she ate or drank. She half-jokingly said that her nickname when she was a child was "Toxie." One could begin to draw a connection between a deep sadness and guilt for causing her mother such distress at birth, and her own adult allergies. The disturbance was extended when the mother and babe could not be together because the mother was hospitalized and so ill. In simple terms, they couldn't bond. For Jane, this completion of the reaching out movement was tremendously relieving and generated a great healing for her.

The interruption at birth is perhaps more common than any research would indicate. More than just severe medical conditions and circumstances, there are entire generations of us who were born to mothers who were unconscious, drugged so heavily that they didn't know the sex of their child until hours later. I can only speculate at the effect of this chemical and medical intervention in the birth process on our current state of social disconnect. One of my favorite thinkers, Joseph Chilton Pearce, has studied this subject extensively, and I highly recommend his book, *Evolution's End*, to those interested in looking more deeply into the subject of the neurological development of the child.

Things to Consider

For this topic, I've chosen not to include an actual exercise. These early separations can cause a very primal and heartrending grief that is often buried in the business of life. It would be better to work on early interruption issues with a trained professional.

You can, however, check the facts and find out if there were any problems at your birth. The reality is that many of us, including myself, were born to heavily drugged mothers. Others had a lot of medical intervention and many current medical processes continue to interfere with that important moment of infant-mother bonding.

Did you or your mother suffer any illness or medical emergencies that caused a prolonged separation either at birth or within the first year of your development?

Were there any severe stresses on your mother prior to your birth? This would include a C-section as sometimes this form of entry into the world can cause a child to feel a bit like, "How did I get here?"

Whatever your answers are to some of these questions, we can only call them fate or perhaps "karma" and acknowledge that these early factors have somehow contributed to your development. This is not always an adverse reaction but can cause you to develop into the kind of person who pays close attention to the feelings of others and their needs.

Exercise 1

The one small exercise that can ease the effects of early interruptions is to perhaps sit in meditation and to imagine yourself holding an infant you in your arms and rocking, singing, and speaking sweetly to the newborn. This simple exercise can bring such a healing connection and is well worth doing.

You will want to make sure you stay the mothering figure for this little one, so all fears and insecurities are cradled firmly in your arms. Often when I have had clients do this exercise, they will notice that tears well up and the heart is touched. This is frozen grief thawing out, and the tears are tears of relief, so do allow them.

Separating From the Parents Successfully

In the literature about child-rearing there is much information about the natural pulling away from parents and family that begins in adolescence and continues until the child is fully out of the house. The focus is on the movements of the child. I seldom see a discussion on when it is right and appropriate for the parents to also separate from the child's business.

In some traditional native cultures, the Elders also teach the parents how to let the child go. While doing the research for my book on adolescence, The Lonely Place, I discovered that one of the most important elements of the rite of passage rituals is the separation phase, where the child goes to the mountain, into the sweat lodge, or on a journey alone. This is for the child's benefit, to break the familiar childhood patterns and open up the universe, but it is also for the benefit of the parents, particularly the mother. She must see her little one go off to become a man or woman.

When there are heavy entanglements, we often can't see how our patterns are playing out in the child. Unfortunately, we attempt to complete our own flawed development through them. This tendency is more frequent than many realize. Does the child go off to college to learn and determine his own life, or does he go off to college to satisfy unfinished business with mom or dad?

Naturally, we want our children to succeed in life, but the reality is that they must go out and break their own hearts a dozen—or a million times—in order to gain the strength and flexibility to figure it out. Sheltering them from life can't achieve this. As parents, we have our fate. As children, we have our fate. The two are not related.

The hidden orders of love dictate that each person must carry his or her own fate and whatever it contains. When one person's fate is mistaken for another, we have entanglement.

The flow of life is downward from one generation to the next. As parents we need to assist this downward flow in all ways possible. From the first year and onward we can begin to let our child solve his own problems in as many ways as possible. When we intervene and do it *for* them, we block or even remove developmental opportunities for growth. Children

37

need to solve complex problems in order for the brain to stretch and grow and to set the stage for later, more complex development.

For instance, my daughter was very shy in early adolescence. She found conflict of any kind difficult and didn't like to have to face uncomfortable situations. I saw that this pattern was familiar to my own patterns. Rather than taking on more and more of her necessary tasks (to save her any discomfort), I began to push her to deal with small tasks herself—simple things like needing new contact lenses but not wanting to call the doctor's office to order them. She still has a tendency toward shyness, but she can now be appropriately mouthy when she needs to be.

We cannot shelter our children from life itself. While they are in our sphere, we give all we can, and then we need to let them separate and go forward. Just as we need to accept our parents as they are, we also need to accept our children as they are. Stay out of their business when at all possible.

One day a client called to talk to me about her nearly-fifteen-year-old son. She was considering putting him into therapy because she was finding little secretive signs that the son was interested in sex. Now, there may have been heavier issues of which I was not aware, but I hung up the phone smiling. I told my husband about the call, and he said from age fifteen on he could think of nothing but sex.

We have to be careful about trying to *cure* our children of normal developmental movements. In order to become functioning adults, they need to learn to manage anger, indecision, sadness, conflict, sexuality, and a huge host of other life situations—and they need to manage them without us. Parenting is a two-edged sword. We must judge what are normal developmental humps and bumps and what may have more serious underlying entanglements. We can be better parents when we have cleared our own developmental issues and taken our own life to its fullest. A later chapter is devoted to parenting, but in this section you should question whether your own separation from your parents is complete. If you are in your mid-twenties or beyond, you should feel a clear separation between the affairs of your parents and your own..

Exercise 1
Testing for Ancestral Strength

1. Choose one of your special objects to represent each of your parents and one for yourself.

2. This time instead of having your representative object face the parents, have the object facing forward with the parents at your back.

3. If you want, you can choose an object for a goal or vision that you have for your life such as starting a business, finishing a new degree, or whatever. Place it slightly "out of reach" and then have the object that is representing you move slowly toward that future goal.

4. Now check your energy gauge and see if the movement feels easy or if there is a pull from either parent to stay within their sphere. The ideal picture would be you facing forward with the strength of your family and lineage behind you.

Again, this is not a solution but a way to determine the hidden energies that may exist within the family. If there is an urge to return to the parents, there may be an entanglement with either parent or someone behind them. We will explore more of this later. Remember that the goal of constellation work is to free your energies so that you can easily move forward into all that you want from life.

When the Adult Child Cannot Separate

I have observed that there is a strong correlation between personal happiness and the attitudes and opinions we hold toward our parents. The most disordered and disturbed individuals I've worked with are those who'vee decided that they somehow got *the wrong parents*. One of my constellation trainers said that the child who despises the parent will punish himself. Another said that if we want to know how somebody's life is going, we can tell by his or her attitude toward the parents. It's in this primary point of connection to the source of our own lives that a schism or split may occur. The head says one thing—but the soul says something else.

Early on in my first marriage, my husband and I both entered a treatment program that was based on the 12-Step Program of Alcoholics Anonymous. We were both quickly labeled "adult children of alcoholics" and "codependent." I accepted the diagnosis because I'd struggled for so many years with a history of sadness, depression, and loneliness that I could never explain. There were many times when I couldn't rise from my bed until early afternoon, and even that was accomplished only by pushing or punishing myself. I felt listless and lifeless. I wanted an answer. Like others, I wanted to know what could have happened to make my life so miserable.

We finished treatment and began attending 12-Step meetings and did so for many years. Eventually, I searched every dusty corner for what my parents had *done wrong*. In a way I rejected my family of origin and surrounded myself with my new recovery family where I felt safe and loved by many.

In hindsight, this was a particularly pathological time for me. I began to despise my parents for not doing it right. I saw my mother as weak and my father as absent and distant. I named them both alcoholics (although I had never even seen them drunk). This went on for a number of years as I held my head above my parents and looked down at them. They both sensed my criticism and it was painful for them. This too-big attitude was also hurtful and confusing to my siblings as I tried to pull them into my new worldview. Finally, it was also damaging to my soul—because I deeply love my parents.

In a movement far too common in the 12-step and therapy worlds, I bought my membership into the recovery program at a heavy price to my own soul—a price that was injurious to the deeper membership in my family of origin. This is a typical conflict between what the brain/mind has decided and what the deeper soul knows. To be in the recovery program meant accepting the recovery world beliefs and philosophies or risk being pushed out.

At the time I was studying Neurolinguistic Programming (NLP) and advancing rapidly as a speaker, teacher, and writer. As I grew and progressed, some of my friends seemed to withdraw from me. They made snide remarks about my success and acted small and jealous. It seemed that my 12-step friends supported my pain beautifully—but knew nothing about how to support my success or growth. It seemed that to keep my membership in this program, I must stay in pain.

When, after many years, I started wanting more than endless meetings and drunkalogues and parent-bashing, I left the recovery program. Even then I heard rumors that I had relapsed and lost the path of recovery. However, the ties to my family proved to be stronger and deeper than the surface ties to my friends in the program. I took a new path toward meditation and yoga and turned my attention inward for the next decade.

I'm grateful that my relationship with my parents was fully restored before they both died. In retrospect, I'm also grateful for the time I spent in the recovery programs. It gave me time to grow, try on new behaviors, and learn to make friends more easily. This was an important but confusing time for me.

The 12-step programs are an example of a social system with its own orders for belonging and membership. Our culture has many of these: school systems, clubs, jobs, college, etc. and each system has its own set of rules for belonging. Most of these we live within nicely, never coming into conflict with the deeper systems of family. Others cause a conflict that increases our level of disturbance.

Separating from parents and the family of origin is a natural and sometimes painful stage of development. Ideally, this separation process begins in mid-to-late adolescence and continues until it is complete, and we are freely belonging to our own new system. Hellinger says that this separation causes a guilt—how can I leave them behind when they have given so much? This guilt is part of the separation process and we must accept it. The guilt is naturally resolved when we make life go forward into the next generation or find other ways to contribute to our society.

Hopefully, we have separated from our parents before we choose a mate. However, there are often invisible threads tugging us back into our system of origin and we become entangled and unable to make the break. Essentially, when this happens, we are stuck in adolescence or childhood. Robert Bly, in his book, *The Sibling Society*, states that we have become a society comprised of mostly adolescent adults. We stay at home well into our thirties or forties or beyond and are somehow unable to fully separate. This failure to separate, in my experience with others, is one of the most common causes of emotional and even physical disorders.

Our culture contributes to this delayed development by overly sheltering and protecting our young people. We don't allow them to take risks, form their own identities, and move forward toward adult development. Likewise, our schools operate from the premise of routine and regimentation and emphasize performance rather than real learning.

Ideally, the goal of every parent is to prepare his or her child to separate from the family of origin. Simultaneously, we want them to be able to draw on the strength and wisdom of their Elders and the lineage. When we become entangled in the fate of earlier family members, we are caught in a loop of coming and going, pulling away and drawing back. If we can see the entanglement, as we are able to in a constellation, and understand that we have no right to carry the fate of others, then we can separate with love and respect, thus gaining full freedom.

In my case, I learned through this work that my chronic sadness and depression were feelings I carried for my mother. Her father had died when she was a young teen, and I don't think she ever got over missing him. I was entangled in her sadness and grief and *this* was the cause of my ongoing depression. Now, as a mental exercise, I place my mother with her father (my grandfather) and see her come to light in a beautiful way. This frees me from her sadness and allows me to stand alone as an adult woman.

Often, when we are unable to separate, we take the route of turning parents into perpetrators, thus justifying a kind of butcher knife approach to separation. This unfortunate trend is sometimes assisted by many of the psychological or therapeutic models currently available. When adult life is not working, we look *back in time* to see who treated us poorly—or we take a therapist as a replacement for the parent. This can only end in additional dependency—and not personal growth and advancement.

By understanding and accepting the natural orders of love within the family, we are able to step outside of this childlike way of seeing, and view the family from a much larger perspective. Now we can see the extreme burdens and entanglements that may have kept the parents revolving in such a destructive vortex—and we can leave it with them. It's as if we are standing on a hilltop looking out across the landscape of our family, but we can see above the trees and valleys to what lies below. This is not the same as getting too big and judging or criticizing. This is a wide view seen with adult eyes.

In these moments, with this extended view, something hard and crusty melts away. The love deep in the soul reemerges and we see, finally, that our parents, too, were children serving their parents and family with blind love and loyalty. This doesn't excuse bad parenting or abusive family dynamics, but it can release us from the entanglement.

Parents don't set out to be bad parents. Nobody rubs her swollen belly while thinking of all the ways it is possible to mess up her child. Parents who are heavily burdened as adults become bad parents. In some tribal societies, it was often the grandparents who raised the children both because the young parents were needed to gather and prepare food—but also because the Elders recognized that the young parents didn't have enough skill or wisdom to do a good job with the little ones.

Since I began studying constellation work, it is now clear that if we have a body and are alive, our parents must have done *something* right. One night I was working with a client who was stuck in her story that her parents didn't give her anything. I was feeling mouthy that night and reminded her that her parents didn't put her in a bag with a heavy rock and drop her in the river like an unwanted kitten. They must have done something right or she wouldn't be alive.

Despite public opinion and current thought, there is little research to support the idea that coming from a dysfunctional family necessarily scars the individual for life. Quite to the contrary, some research supports the idea that often these children grow up to be more flexible, courageous, and resilient than those that grow up in families that are too generous and loving.

Sadly, the butcher knife approach to separation from parents seldom works. It cuts into the soul and does its bloodletting there because, deep within our childlike soul, we love our parents no matter what. If we are programmed by our society to despise our parents for what they did to us, we come into severe conflict within our own soul and the system of origin. We begin to adopt the narrative stories such as, "My dad was an abusive drunk. My mom was a doormat. They had no time for me. I didn't get what I needed. I never got a thing from them." Soon this narrative becomes the tape loop running our lives. If you listen carefully to these loops, you will hear a small, whiny (and grieving) child. The irony of this is that people running these tape loops are often doing to themselves what was done initially—ignoring their own needs and desires and blaming others. In essence, the pattern has become self-perpetuating thus creating irresolvable conflict structures within. We become our own perpetrator.

Paradoxically, all the judgments placed upon the shoulders of the parent causes the adult child to remain even more firmly tied and entangled. In these constant refrains from clients I hear only that he is knotted firmly within the system of origin and cannot go on without resolution of the systemic issues.

In viewing the larger system or soul of the family itself, we can see that a severe disturbance has occurred in an earlier generation. The child is not entitled to judge or criticize in this way. The bitter child has rejected and negated the very source of life itself.

It is a tricky ground we tread here because parents are not always innocent in the way I eventually saw that my parents were. Bad things do happen. Sexual abuse, alcoholism, and physical abuse are all too often part of the big picture of family life. It's not the goal of this work to condone those behaviors in any way. We must all be accountable for what we have done or perpetrated upon another. However, strength comes when we simply acknowledge what has occurred and go on from there.

Things to Consider

Families are full of stories. Some are truth, others are rumors, and others are blankets to cover grief, pain, or terrible secrets. Our current culture seems to give children an over-inflated sense of entitlement—as if just being a child means we deserve to have all good things lavished on us. My early trainers have said that children who are given too much feel a deep sense of guilt in their souls. Life itself is such a gift that for parents to give above and beyond upsets the balance of give and take. We will explore this more deeply later, but consider your own attitudes about life and toward your parents. Residual anger can often mask an entanglement.

Exercise 1
Examine the Following Questions.

To gain more understanding about what may be keeping you from designing the life you want, explore the following questions.

1. Do I hold anger at one or both of my parents?

2. What beliefs are at the root of that anger?

3. Have I separated from my parents, or do I spend more time looking at them and not at my own future?

4. Do I feel strong and self-reliant in my life? Am I able to set goals and move at a steady, realistic pace toward those goals?

5. Do I have a tendency to blame others for my failings and faults, or am I able to pick up and carry my own fate and choose a direction for my life?

6. Am I a whiner? Do I constantly complain or point fingers when things are not going well. If so, how can I quit such child-like behavior and become an adult?

Accepting the Parents—As They Are

Forgiveness is touted as a virtue; "To err is human, to forgive divine." However, consider what happens when we decide to forgive someone. We give absolution like a being from on high—as though we had that right and that ability. If we consider the natural flow of energy from one generation to another, we find that forgiveness is not always a good goal. If a child takes the position of *forgiving* the parent for past actions and transgressions, the child is out of order along the generational line—his head is higher than those who came before.

As we restore order within the soul of the family, we discover that a child has no right to forgive the parents. To forgive we must first judge the state of right or wrong and, when we judge our parents, we become too big and powerful thus losing our place in the right order of things. Our goal is to stay free of the burdens of guilt, sadness, or anger that the parents carry.

Another way that we fail to separate is when we leave the family of origin but go on to recreate the system of origin within our new adult system. When our development with the parents is incomplete, we often duplicate it in our adult lives. We discover that we have married mom or dad. This is more common than many of us want to admit. In our early development we may have learned to despise one or both parents and are determined to never be like them. When I hear this in clients, it's always a clue that the person is on course to be exactly like the parent they despise. Out of childlike loyalty, they will either become the despised parent—or marry him or her.

Finally, one more way that we fail to separate is to simply not do it. The child, now in an adult body, remains a child within the care and influence of the parents. These individuals live at home or stay close by. They eat mom's cooking, take care of dad's chores, may never marry, and essentially remain children. This is perhaps the deepest entanglement of all, when we agree simply not to grow and go forward in order to please the parents or to satisfy an entanglement with the parents or some other member of the system.

In order to gain our adult strength in the world, we accept the parents as they are, taking what they gave and determining to find for ourselves what they didn't or couldn't give. This is the stance of health and strength. To better understand this, we can separate out mother and father to see what it is we seek from both.

Things to Consider

You have completed a first fact-finding interview about your family of origin. You have also done a first constellation exercise with both of your parents. Then you did a little self-examination. Now it is time to dig a bit more deeply and excavate old feelings of anger, guilt, or sadness. Most of these old energies are just that—they belong to a much younger you and have locked into your neural networks in a way that may not be serving you or your future goals.

I remember watching Hellinger do a constellation with a male client once who was extremely angry at his father. The man arrived at a place in the constellation where he could at last have seen his father from adult eyes and seen the many ways that his father was burdened, but at the critical moment, the man folded up his arms and said emphatically that he would have nothing to do with his father. Period.

If I remember correctly the man was facing serious health issues that Hellinger felt were connected to this refusal to accept life from "that bastard." Hellinger said something about how the man would rather die than accept his father as he is.

Most of the harsh anger we feel at our parents is really grief. The small child inside still wonders why mother or father couldn't love or accept him. Anger is safer to feel than numbing grief or the idea that we may not be loveable. Remember that you do not have to forgive. This false energy keeps you out of order and bigger than the forces that gave you life. You can, however, see the many burdens that mother or father carried and accept that that was their fate and not your fault. We can honor the fact that mother and father held it together long enough to give us life—and that may have to be enough.

Exercise 1
Seeing From Your Adult Eyes

This exercise comes more from my NLP training than constellation work, but it can be very effective in helping you to see the world from adult eyes and not the wounded eyes of a child. If you feel a stubborn refusal of either parent or the unwillingness to entertain the idea that he or she was burdened and entangled, then try the following exercise.

1. From your bowl of constellation objects, take three objects. One will represent the small injured you, and the other will represent the older and wiser part that such a history has given you. You will also want to choose a representative for the parent that you are struggling with.

2. First put the little you facing the big you. Now, tell that little one that you are learning to stay your right age and that you will never, ever let anybody hurt the little you again. You are making a solemn promise to develop the life strategies that will insure that the little you will not be ignored or shoved aside ever again. You may even ask the little one (or sense) what he or she needs from you. Be open to whatever comes to you. It may be a request for ice cream.

3. When the little one feels sufficiently secure in your promise (and please, do not make this promise lightly), then you may turn to the parents and in your best adult voice, say the following sentence.

> "Dear Mother (or Father). I recognize that your life carried heavy burdens and that this younger me was not responsible for these burdens. This little part of me was innocent on all accounts and did nothing to deserve poor treatment. Now, I acknowledge you as the source of my life, but the care of this little one now

belongs to me. All burdens that belong to you, I return to you now in respect for what you suffered."

Note that again this is just the beginning of learning how to pay attention to and care for the younger parts of yourself. When you make this promise, it means you can no longer call yourself stupid or silly or other names. You can no longer ignore your own needs. Often what happens when the parenting was less than it should have been is that we begin to act like the offending parent and do to ourselves what was done initially.

Exercise 2
Taking the Strength of Your Lineage

If you feel that you have successfully separated from your parents and are now standing firmly in your own adult life, you can still benefit by strengthening your connection to both the line of mother and father. Even though both of my parents were deceased by the time I was introduced to the constellation work, I have since learned to go often to the "well" of my parents and have a little sip. This meditation can assist you with that.

1. When you are facing a difficult decision or feeling unsupported in your adult life, take yourself off to a quiet space and sit in a comfortable chair or your meditation space.

2. Imagine yourself alone in a vast meadow surrounded by mountains.

3. In your arms are the many burdens you have accumulated over the past many weeks or months. Each burden is a stone and is heavy and cold. Your arms are weary from carrying the weight of these many things.

4. You walk across the meadow to the foothills of two gigantic mountains and in one you see the female form and in the other the male form. These are not just your parents but the mother and father of all, more spirit than physical body.

5. Lay down the many stones you have been carrying and then, one by one, pick up one of the stones and tell the two mountains what you have been struggling with.

6. Ask them for their support in making your burdens lighter. You may notice that you are more strongly drawn to one or the other of the two mountains,

either the female or the male. Lay your burden down before whichever you are drawn.

7. Thank them for helping you to bear these burdens and then make a slight bow and leave the stones with them. As you walk away, you can feel the strength emanating from these towering mountains and you feel stronger because they are behind you now.

Aging Parents and Elders

One of my favorite movements within the constellation is the image of a single person facing forward toward the future with all of their parents and grandparents and ancestors at his or her back. Often when a client has finished the work, I have them stand a moment with this array of ancestors behind them and remind them that the two lineages to which they belong extend back thousands and thousands of years. When the client allows this energy to come forward into his or her body, the feeling is one of tremendous strength.

Modern culture has somehow lost touch with this simple reality. Instead of taking the wisdom of our Elders, we use the world "elderly" or "seniors." It's amazing how different these words feel.

It would benefit us greatly to take note of how some tribal native societies deal with the Elders. During our long adventures into Indian country as we produced the native music documentaries, Milt and I were constantly amazed at the reverent respect offered the living Elders and the ancestors. Often we could not even record the music without permission from the Elders. And if they did not agree—we did not record. The Elders in some of Indian Country are truly the backbone of the culture. Other Native communities have taken their ancestors suffering as their own—and they do not heal.

In different healthy cultures all over the world, the ancestors and deceased are honored with food, shrines, prayer rituals, and special honoring spaces in the home. Even in our immigrant society, we should reinstate this practice of honoring the Elders and the deceased ancestors through family ritual and prayer.

It is through the grandparents and great-grandparents that life comes to us, our parents and then to our children and grandchildren. This makes them sacred—regardless of what tough blows life has dealt them.

As a child I had one grandmother who I didn't like very much and, frankly, I don't think she liked me. She had wild, red, painted hair, bright lipstick, and she drank beer all day long. She also grew the best strawberries. I was afraid of her and she chased me outside whenever we visited.

It wasn't until I came to this systemic work that I began to recall and see things in a different light. I recalled that her father, my great-grandfather, came from Denmark. I only knew him as a very old man (in his 90s) who used to smile toothlessly and feed us lemon drops when we came to see him. He lived in an apartment on my grandparents' small farm. My grandmother lovingly cared for him until he died at age 97.

Now, as I take these principles and place them fully in my heart, I see only that this woman, my grandmother, carried my own father in her womb for nine months and made his life possible—and so made my life and the lives of my children possible. This is a debt I can never repay.

An odd shift of perception and awareness happens as we move through our own life stages from child to parent to grandparent. When I first wrote these words, I was in Lincoln, Nebraska, awaiting the birth of my twin granddaughters and thinking often of my own mother. I wondered if she also worried and fretted when I, her daughter, was pregnant and about to give birth. During those quiet days of waiting for the twins, I was like a shape-changer constantly shifting from child to parent to expectant grandparent. It was like moving through holes in time—one minute this, another minute that.

When parents or grandparents become aged and ill it is sometimes difficult to continue to see them as adults and the very source of our life. They may have lost certain capacities and are in need of care. In these moments we must be careful not to switch into parenting them and lose our perspective as children. Elder parents and grandparents always hold a place *above* us in the generational flow.

Our transient culture sometimes puts thousands of miles between a young family and its Elders. The little ones never have the opportunity to benefit from the wisdom and experience of those who came before.

Americans are perhaps a unique culture in that all of the early (and current) immigrant families experience a break or a cutting off from relatives and traditions. Additionally, the Native people who were her first often feel like they have lost their place in our culture.

When Milt and I flew to Germany once to interview Bert Hellinger, he told us, "Americans are restless—they seek their relatives." He also said that we need to come to terms with the American holocaust, where millions of native people died, and see that this new America offered refuge to millions. There is this—and there is that.

My parents and grandparents never spoke much about our ancestors or our original homelands. It was as if we were dropped onto the earth near Cass Lake, Minnesota without any ties to any other place. When my mother died, my seven siblings and I were left the task of sorting out her life and belongings. It was both painful and pleasurable, but what I noticed was that we all sought small signs of how our mother felt about life—what she was curious about, what pleased her, etc. Our greatest find was a small, wire-bound recipe book in which she had written one recipe card about each of our births. That tiny little book made us all weep as we read it.

As Americans, it may be especially important for us to look into where we came from, and to take back what we have lost. This may explain the Celtic movement, the Scottish groups, even the New Age trend to try to identify with Indians.

Exercise 1
Things to Consider

The following things to consider could also be treated as exercises. Make a regular practice of checking in with yourself to see how you are doing.

1. Separate the Soul from the Action. Realize that the soul of the parent or grandparent is still intact regardless of what they carried, and that they were strong enough to pass life on to you and allow the life to grow. See the soul and not just the action. Sometimes it is useful to consider your mother and father as images beyond the body, almost a mystical force that acted as the living container that poured life into your body. What happens deep within the soul of the individual looks very different than what happens on the physical level of events and action.

2. Maintain the Right Order. With your parents, be a child. With your children, be a parent. Maintain the right order. Be alert to the temptation to treat those who are above you as if they are below. In too many families the children are parenting the parents and the elders are set aside as useless. The generational orders are important to maintaining the right balance and flow of energy.

3. Speak Kindly of Those Who Came Before You. Respect your relatives and ancestors, especially to your own children. Let them know they are linked through time and space to a long unbroken lineage. Pay particular attention to any members who were distanced by the family, for instance an aunt who was placed in an institution or an uncle who died drunk on a highway. Refrain from all scorn or ridicule of any earlier members of your system. For instance, when I saw my grandmother in the new light of this work, I suddenly realized that out of all my ancestors, I was most like this

56

particular grandmother. It made me laugh, and I suddenly felt great kindness for her and found a picture of her and told her, "Grandmother, I am just like you!" We were both addicted to novels, loved to garden, raised fruit, and liked to bake.

4. Look into Your Personal History. Discover where your families came from. Do genealogy searches or hunt old letters to find and collect family stories. If there are still Elders within your reach, record them and ask them questions about their lives. Share these with your children so they feel the links and ties to the ancestors. In particular, seek out the important events or early deaths, etc. that may have impacted family members who came before you. I am always amazed at how often a client has a *crazy* aunt or uncle or somebody who was born retarded and shunted off somewhere. We want to have our eyes and hearts open especially toward these excluded members.

5. 5. Acknowledge the past. You might even write letters of thank-you to your ancestors—especially any with whom you feel a special affinity. If you discover a relative who was excluded for some reason, give them a special place in your heart. Creating a family tree does the same thing, giving each member his or her proper place within the flow of time.

6. Drink from both cups of the family. An enriching exercise may be to actually pour some nourishing drink into two cups and then drink from them both. One represents your father's line, the other your mother's line.

7. Examine your personal stories or social programs—and question them thoroughly. What other systems do you belong to, and what are their rules and orders? Do they conflict with what your

deeper soul or self understands or longs to understand? If you feel disconnected from the source of your life (mother and father) you may be more vulnerable to choosing groups that offer to replace mom and dad. When you have outgrown your chosen group's rules or regulations—move on. Find a new group. It is human nature to develop and outgrow friends, jobs, churches, and other social groups. Be willing to find a better fit.

8. Create an honoring space in your house for grandparents and ancestors. We can move toward deeply honoring the source of our lives when we create a sacred space in our home that honors our parents and relatives with pictures, mementos or other symbolic items. If no photos are available we can use small stones or objects to hold a place. A friend of mine told me a story about how she was going through a rough period in her life and was very drawn to a grandmother that she couldn't even remember. Without any knowledge of this work or its principles, she decided to bring her grandmother closer into view. The grandmother had raised African violets and had over 200 plants in her house at her death. My friend went out and bought a few violets and tended them, watered them, and even talked to her grandmother through them. This exercise brought her grand-mother's energy forward and allowed her to connect with it.

Exercise 2
Practice Gratitude

One time I listed all the ways I was grateful to my parents. I called this "A thousand thank-yous." It was a healing and gentle exercise. If we do this with an open and receptive heart, we may even find gratitude for the times of struggle and conflict—they are often the source of our greatest strengths.

1. Tell your parents either silently or verbally, "Without you, I would not live. For this I am indebted to you forever and I thank you. My life comes from you."

2. Push your brain to remember the small gestures or moments in which the love did flow in your family. Recall that small pat on the shoulder, the loving glance, and the quiet moments. Release some of the lesser memories and stories that you have accepted as true. Sometimes when we are doing inner work we are looking for trouble and may be overlooking the memories of strength and connection that we also received.

3. Write your own "A Thousand Thank-Yous".

Exercise 3
Meditate on Your Place

1. Sit quietly in meditation and imagine parents, grandparents, and great-grandparents from both sides standing behind you like a powerful range of mountains in which you are simply the "foot hill."

2. Silently invite or ask them to bless you and give you what strength they have so that you can go forward.

Exercise 4
Ask for Help

One of my trainers told a wonderful story about a man who imagined a theater filled with his ancestors with the most recent members occupying the front rows. He would go into the theater and stand before them and pose his problems and ask for their help. If serious events have weakened the ancestral line, stretch further back until you find the unbroken line. I have turned this example into a simple exercise for you to try.

1. Take the issue you are struggling with and imagine yourself walking into a theater that is filled with the many generations of ancestors behind you. Your parents are in the first row, your grandparents in the second, and as the theater rows rise behind them, more and more ancestors are present.

2. Tell them about what you are struggling with. Admit that you are just a younger member of this lineage, and that you need their strength and wisdom.

3. When you have posed your request, simply thank them and let them know that you will be watching for the correct solution and know that it will come.

Going Beyond Your Parents or Ancestors

Early in my own personal work, I mentioned to my trainer, Heinz that I sometimes felt as if there was a ceiling on what it was possible for me to do or be. This ceiling seemed to have little or no connection to my own talent, abilities, or intelligence but seemed to come from somewhere else. What he said to me in his playful German accent stirred another profound truth about being a child in my family. He said, "The hardest thing you will ever do is to exceed your own parents."

His words struck a note inside of me. My father was very creative and inventive, but he had little formal education. It stopped him from advancing in his work although he became entrepreneurial. My mother had gone to a secretarial school but essentially her entire adult life was to be mother to all of us. Education was not pushed in my family. As an adult, I was the only one of eight children to get a four-year college degree and, when I entered a graduate program the first time, it became so uncomfortable that I dropped out. It was a strange and frustrating time for me. I now realize why I couldn't complete the graduate program—I remained loyal to my father and mother.

The hidden loyalty in the soul of a child can act like a thick glass-ceiling ending where our parents left off. We can often see clearly what is beyond the barrier, but can't seem to go through it. It is not the parents' intention to place this ceiling—it happens automatically as we remain blindly loyal to our parents and their station in life. We can suffer a deep sense of guilt when we step beyond their boundaries. It's as if the soul were asking, "How can I have so much if my parents could not?"

Moving on or beyond the parents or grandparents requires that we resolve our entanglements and move to a place where we see the parents as children within their own family systems. In this state of conscious love, we can see our parents more clearly and understand that they are pleased by our success. We can even say to them in our minds, "Please bless me when I go beyond you. In this way, I honor the life you gave me." Instead of maintaining a kind of blind childlike loyalty, we go forward and honor the gift they gave us—our life—by doing well.

In my travels and work in Indian country, I can see that a hundred-plus years of oppression of American Indian people has lowered the ceiling to a dangerous level. With poverty, high unemployment, and a statistically low level of education, the ceiling is a few feet off the ground for many native families. If the children of these families remain blindly loyal to their parents, the motivation to achieve is compromised. It is as if there is an unwritten agreement to not succeed that is made even more complex by American history. Sometimes success can mean that the white man won. The solution to this can be found in the simple sentence, "In honor of all that you have suffered, I will make my life rich and meaningful. I do this for you."

Just after I began a graduate program (again) in 2001, I was talking to my sister who also has this glass ceiling. She told me about an important meeting she'd attended with many highly educated people. Because she has only an AA degree, she felt shy and uncomfortable and wondered what she was doing there. However, as the meeting came to a close, she realized that most of the ideas adopted by the committee had come from her! We were having this conversation on the phone and I said, "Try this. Make a picture of Dad in front of you and then ask him 'Dad, please bless me when I go beyond you'".

She immediately felt the emotional impact of those words in her soul and said, "That is so powerful."

A little later I was working with another therapist in an unusual technique he uses to connect clients with their parents and ancestors. At one point he told me to visit my father in the other realms and to ask him something important. I saw my father clearly in my mind, and I felt sad that none of his inventions ever flowered. In my mind, my father laughed at me and said simply, "This is not true. I *invented* you, didn't I?" Somehow this simple exchange made me laugh and gave me a greater permission to go on. Eventually I even finished graduate school.

When my siblings or I succeed, it proves that my father's *inventions* did work. When we do well, it honors his life and the fathering of eight very creative children. As a testament to this, I recall that my father was married on June 18, had his first child on June 18, and died on June 18 with all eight of us around him—and it was Father's Day. His life was about inventing us.

Again, to cross the family barriers and surpass the ceiling, we need to see our parents clearly and acknowledge whatever fate or circumstances they may have suffered. We need to see them not with the blind loyalty of a child but with the conscious love of an adult. When we have fully taken our proper place as a child of our system and honored the gift of life that came from our parents, and from the greater force beyond, only then can we move clearly and cleanly into our next roles as partners, parents, and grandparents.

As you read these words, notice whether you resist the proposition that we must take our parents as they are before life can go on in a good way. I know from experience that some of you will want to clutch your beliefs tightly, hold to your stories, and demand that your parents did it wrong—and that is why you suffer. Be careful. Take notice. This conflict will keep you small, stuck in a childlike way of viewing the world. Your soul is in conflict because at the base of belief and being, we know that without our parents we would have no life. When we turn our backs on that source of life, we are in trouble.

An image I like to use in workshops is to have people visualize a great, crystal-clear reservoir high up in the mountains. This reservoir contains all the energy of our ancestors as well as the great and unknowable forces of God or the universe or Creator, etc. When a child is created, two gates open and this immense life force begins spilling out from the great reservoir and begins flowing down the mountain. The gates, of course, are mother and father. The water begins to cut a course and becomes a river or a stream flowing downward. When we become adults, the "flow" of our river depends on how much of that water continues to flow down and out of the reservoir. If the gates (of the two parents) are not fully open, we will not have the flow we need. These are sacred gates that exist beyond the more mundane reality of who did what to whom. When we see this sacred quality, we can acknowledge whatever difficult fate our parents suffered and still let the water flow down and out.

Oddly, this vision of the great reservoir has also helped me to understand why so often a person's best efforts fail. Many of my clients or friends are working frantically down river, using therapy, affirmations, positive thinking, reading self-help, hiring coaches—desperately trying to rearrange the river banks when the problem is the flow coming out of the reservoir.

Being the child in the system of origin is sometimes difficult. Stuff happens. On the one hand we are not *entitled* to carry any burdens of sadness or guilt for our parents or ancestors. On the other hand, a deep soul loyalty makes us want to pick up and carry their pain and loss. It is a two-edged sword.

The only thing that softens these simple truths is when, in a constellation, we see that ancestor or parent carry the consequences of his own actions and his own suffering. He gains a sure measure of strength and dignity from having withstood such a fate, and we can see this unfold within the constellation. Hellinger says that when we bravely bear what has happened, our soul gains weight. It is also clear in the constellation that there is no relief to the parents or ancestors when the dead see the younger members suffer for them. It is best for all when each member of the system carries his or her own portion.

One client I worked with had lost her husband to suicide. Jenny was beset by guilt and sadness, nearly crazy with it. In a very powerful and emotional constellation, she at last left the act (of suicide) with her husband and went to stand with her children. There is no way to describe the strength that flowed from that representational act. Both her husband and Jenny were strengthened by it.

In an early training seminar with Heinz Stark that my husband Milt and I both attended, Heinz expressed a sincere interest to visit the Pine Ridge Reservation to introduce the constellation work there. He had the idea that the descendants of those who died in the Wounded Knee Massacre were bravely trying to carry the pain for those who had died—and were continuing the suffering as a result.

This form of love and carrying for earlier members takes the dignity away from those who suffered such a fate, and it disrupts the soul of the family. Also, when such an event causes the next generations attempt to bear such unspeakable pain and loss, the dead cannot rest peacefully because the grandchildren suffer so.

Since we knew many people on the reservation, Milt and I agreed to take him down the next day. We spontaneously put him on KILI FM Radio and held a constellation demonstration that night. It was very powerful. We later returned with Heinz several times to continue the work there. Looking into the systemic effects of catastrophic historical events could take a lifetime of study.

As this satellite of thinking shifts, we see that we are both *linked* and *separate* from our system of origin. When we no longer carry anything for our ancestors, we are free to go forward and form a system of our own—and they are free to carry the weight of their own souls. This freedom and connection is the goal of constellation work.

Things to Consider

As children of our system, we are not entitled to pick up and bear the burdens of those who came before. We must leave it with them. Essentially, it is not our business to interfere or to judge. This is sometimes easier said than done, and our current culture loves to pass blame around like shiny pennies. Practice disconnecting from those who came before you while, at the same time, feeling the lineage of both ancestral lines behind you as was suggested in an earlier exercise. Try the following exercises either with your representative objects, or just do it in your mind.

Exercise 1
Seeking the Blessings of Your Lineage

Repeat these ritual sentences either using representative objects or in a meditation. If your parents are still alive and you feel comfortable doing this, you may ask their blessings directly.

1. "Dear Mother, I ask that you bless me when I go beyond you in my education and life goals. All of this is possible because you have freely given me this life. I thank you and honor you by all that I do. Please bless me when I go forward."

2. "Dear Father, I ask that you bless me when I go beyond you in my education and life goals. All of this is possible because you have freely given me this life. I thank you and honor you by all that I do. Please bless me when I go forward."

Note: If there have been a lot of abusive patterns in your family, you may imagine your mother or father more as sacred beings than physical beings. For instance if you are a Christian, you may envision Jesus and Mother Mary standing behind or beside your parents and honor them. If you had a stronger relationship with your grandparents than your parents, it is fine to place the grandparents behind the parents and honor the entire lineage. It can be difficult to shift your perspective if you have grown up with abuse.

However, it can be much more difficult *not* to shift your perspective and to stay forever entangled in the abusive system. Also, our empirical evidence shows that when abuse goes unresolved, it is much more likely to be passed on to your or your children. The cycle stops when you are released from the entanglement and from the parents but are still able to honor the source of your life and your connection to your lineage.

The Right Place

Most of our exploration so far has been about the parents and grandparents. Before moving into the formation of new systems, we should pause a moment on the relationships between siblings. The sibling line can be a tremendous source of strength for us when the right orders are observed. However, as we have discovered above, changes in the family can scramble the sibling line also. Occasionally we do not know about or are not allowed access to our brothers and sisters. When siblings are not given their right place, the consequences can be troubling for all.

My own family fits an almost ideal picture. I was the third of eight children. There were no known miscarriages, no half brothers or sisters, no children from previous partners, no previous partners, and no early deaths. I'm blessed with the strength I gain from being so closely linked and supported by so many siblings. We don't squabble or compete or fight. My one frustration is that we all seem to share the glass ceiling I mentioned in the previous chapter. I sometimes see great abilities and talents go undeveloped. However, in this instance, I count my blessings—and they number seven.

Many families, however, are not so fortunate. Families become scrambled in dozens of ways. The consequences can result in everything from constant feuding between siblings to individual troubles. My belief (and experience) indicates that siblings missing or unaccounted for in the sibling line can result in depression, illness, weight problems, mental disturbance, gender confusion, withdrawal, general confusion, anger, and even suicide.

Remember from the earlier discussion that a child's place in the family is secured at the moment of conception when the flickering spirit leaves the spirit world and becomes corporeal, or takes physical form. This spiritual law, if we could be so bold in calling it that, cares nothing for circumstances. It doesn't matter whether the two partners who have joined in this sexual union are drunk or married or even related. It doesn't matter whether the conception is convenient, or the mother too young, or if one of the partners happens to be married to somebody else. It simply is. There is no such thing as "safe sex" when we are talking about the natural orders within the family. We bear the consequences of conceiving a child. In fact, it may be that effective birth control methods have caused us to trivialize this most sacred union—the moment when a new life is created.

Regardless of whether the action was done out of profound love or careless entertainment, the consequences once a new life is formed are immediate and lasting.

Children are lost when a father is not told he has conceived a child. Children are lost when miscarriages and abortions are too easily dismissed. Children are lost when they are stillborn or die early, and the pain of the loss is so great the parents cannot think about the child. Children are lost when they are given over to adoption and left to wonder all their lives whether they are brother or sister to others. Whatever the circumstances, the consequences to the soul of the family can be harsh.

There are no rules to follow in terms of how to restore what has been lost. There is also no judgment as long as we carry the consequences of our actions. In the systemic view, the only resolution is to give the missing child back his or her place in the family. This can release any entanglement of the other children. It's as if the remaining children in a sibling line will attempt to hold a place for the missing child. If we can't accomplish this in the real world, we can do it energetically with the constellation. Below are several examples of what we've observed in constellations as a result of missing siblings.

Squabbling Siblings

Often when one or more children in the sibling line are missing, the remaining members will squabble and compete for position with one another. It's as if the squabbling announces that something is not right in the deeper soul of the family. One woman, Julie, reported that she and her sisters fought so badly that they no longer had any contact with one another as adults. It had been four years since she'd seen her youngest sister but, when they got together, it was always one big fight. As we talked she recalled that her father had been married previously. The first wife died birthing a boy who also died three days later. Although Julie knew of this first wife and her son, her father had never talked openly about it. The issue was simply not mentioned.

Julie had never once considered that this dead boy was her older brother. When we set up her constellation, we brought in representatives for the first wife and her son as well as Julie and her three sisters. The response was immediate. The sisters were all very interested in the former wife and the boy. The father could not look at either of them. Julie's mother also refused to look at the woman who had come before her.

In the resolution phase of the constellation, Julie and her sisters honored the father's first wife and welcomed her son (their brother) into the family. There was a touching emotional moment as each of the sisters greeted the missing son who was actually the first-born child of their father. In cases such as this one, it's very important to honor the first wife—it was her death that made the new family possible, and this gives the woman and her child a special, elevated place within the system.

Siblings do not always know if there was a previous partner or a child born to either parent previous to the existing system. Sometimes a father is not even aware of it. While we do not recommend prying into the parents' earlier lives, it sometimes will come to light, or the right moment will come for you to ask. Be free of judgment. You only want to know if you have somehow taken on a burden or tried to step in for the missing sibling.

The Early Death of a Sibling

When a child dies early—in the womb or in first few days or years of life—the space he would have occupied is often closed when the parents or other members of the family simply can't stand the pain of the loss. The subject becomes taboo. This can create a precarious situation for the remaining siblings. A deep loyalty exists between siblings and, when one dies early, the living ones may try to hold a space for the lost one or even follow the deceased one into death. It is as if their soul says, "How can I live when you had to leave? It is too painful and so I will follow you." I have seen this arise in many constellations now and the depth of love and loyalty is astonishing when it becomes visible.

Within the knowing field of the constellation, I've seen living siblings act in a number of different ways when one among them has died very early. Often, it is the sibling that comes after or just before the deceased one who suffers most. Sometimes one sibling will gain an extra 150 pounds—as if the weight itself holds the missing place. Other times living siblings experience illness, depression, or suicidal urges. And still other times, I've seen a living sibling take on the sexuality of a deceased sibling of the opposite sex and become gender-confused. Another manifestation can be the busy, busy person who constantly seems to be doing the work of two. This person often has a missing sibling and seems literally to be living two lives.

A psychologist friend and I have even used constellation to explore disorders like Dissociative Identity Disorder (multiple personality) or schizophrenia to determine whether the identity confusion could be the soul's attempt to make missing siblings visible again within the system. In the cases of severe emotional disorders, sometimes the lost sibling was from a previous generation, and sometimes the child did not die a peaceful death. As my friend and I have worked with these serious disorders, we do so very gently and slowly because the systemic disturbance and disorder can be great, and we do not want the client to suffer any additional harm.

In one example, Patrick approached the constellation work because he was chronically sad and felt out of place in his life. He was an older adult and an accomplished lawyer with much going in his favor. As he talked of his family history prior to the constellation, he revealed that he had had an older brother, a first sibling, who died of complications at birth. His parents named him Patrick and buried him at less than two days old. Many years later the parents had another son—and decided to name him Patrick also. Perhaps they only wanted to honor the missing son or to use a cherished family name, but this was not the result. By giving the second child the name of the deceased first child, the right orders were disturbed and Patrick's confusion and sadness grew out of that.

Children who die early should be given their rightful place (and individually named) within the sibling line. The birth order should be observed as if the deceased child were still present. For instance, if a first child died at birth or even in miscarriage, the second child can only be a second child—and not the first in the birth order.

Gender Confusion

Confusion about sexual identity can sometimes come from lost siblings of the opposite sex. This is a controversial statement and one I would not even make except that I have seen this sexual confusion often in clients. I do not bring it about—the dynamic is already present. This could contribute to a person becoming homosexual, experiencing the urge to cross dress, or otherwise feel out of place in his or her body. Often it is the sibling on either side of the missing sibling who experiences this confusion. It's as if, again, the soul of the child must stretch to fill and hold a place for the missing one. This phenomenon can cross the generations. We often find an aunt, uncle, or other significant family member of the opposite sex who is missing or died early.

For example, Leslie experienced a profound confusion about her life and her sexual identity. She had constant dreams about dead babies that haunted her even in her waking hours. In her family history, we discovered three sets of twin boys in multiple generations which had been lost to miscarriage. Leslie's current family had only daughters. She had been treated for years for mental illness and was on and off psychotropic drugs.

We've seen similar gender confusion with a child who carries the feelings of a parent who has lost a significant first love. One of my clients, Marjorie, had very masculine characteristics and a long history of taking care of mom. In the interview and the later constellation we could see a strong energetic link between Leslie and her mother's first fiancée who died in a terrible car crash one week before their wedding. The mother had never let go of the loss of this first love, and the loving daughter tried to fill his place by taking on the masculine qualities of the lost love.

In constellation work, there is no need to judge or even change life-long patterns and, of course, we cannot change what happened. We have no desire to alter homosexuality or other gender issues but seek only to make clearer the forces at work that determine our life's direction. For many people, gender confusion carries a certain amount of social shame. Discovering entanglements with missing siblings or family member may not alter the behavior, but can bring more peace and understanding. In all of the above examples, a sense of relief and freedom came

74

from placing the missing persons back in their respectful places and honoring them so that younger members no longer unconsciously seek to fill their places.

The Birth Order

A great deal has been learned and written about the power of the birth order within families. Reading about your place in line can be startling and uncanny. It can also be useful when events and circumstances within the family have somehow disturbed the natural birth order. As I mentioned above, when a first sibling dies early and the second comes along, he or she can be confused as to their rightful place in the family.

It's also possible that you may have siblings that you know nothing about, perhaps a brief affair that either parent had earlier that is unknown to you in which a child was conceived and perhaps aborted or given up for adoption. I worked with two brothers in one constellation—both suffering from depression, a vague feeling of being out of place, and an almost obsessive need to do and achieve. There was a rumor in the family that father had an affair with another woman between the two brothers and that another brother was conceived from the affair. We could not find out any definitive information about the missing brother, but both felt his presence in their souls.

One of the saddest clients I've worked with was a homosexual man who said he felt as if he were constantly being buried by life. He reported that he had a twin sister who had suffered a lack of oxygen at birth and was developmentally disabled. At age three the sister was institutionalized, and the brother was forced to go through life without his twin. In every constellation I have facilitated that dealt with twins, there always appears to be a very powerful energetic connection between them. In this case, the soul of the healthy twin seemed to suffer a guilt and sadness about the fate of the other twin. In the constellation, the love was acknowledged, and the guilt and sadness left with fate. By the end of the constellation, the man literally looked ten years younger.

From what we have seen in the constellation, a child who was miscarried or stillborn can have a place in the birth order of the sibling line. There tends to be some variation in how much of a place depending upon how far along the pregnancy was, etc. This needs to be tended to on a case-by-case basis. Also, from what I have seen, the miscarried child often occupies a special place in the hearts of the parents. Losing a child who was wanted is a painful event that is sometimes not properly mourned.

In one constellation I did with a woman named Sarah, there was a stillborn sister who came before her. This sister was not named and was seldom talked about in the family. Sarah, my client, had suffered a low-grade depression most of her life and couldn't seem to lift it. When we placed the stillborn sister beside her, a light came on in her face and the "reunion" between the sisters was sweet and so full of love there was hardly a dry eye in the group. All of her life Sarah had felt as though something was missing. We discovered what it was.

The change for her over the months to follow was permanent and the sweetness stayed. One of the healing sentences that I had her say to her sister was, "Come, I will show you all the beautiful things in the world through my eyes." She later told me that she felt as though she could celebrate things, and be happy now because she could share it with her missing sister.

For some reason, when I work with missing siblings, I often have the missing one say to the living one in a joking voice, especially when it is a younger sibling, "I would have made your life miserable." This humor seems to bring the missing sibling into perspective and often brings a healing jump that tears alone would not make. Most siblings do make each other miserable at various times in life.

Things to Consider

If your parents are still living, ask them if they have ever lost a child that you have not been told about. It is not necessary for them to tell you about abortions or such—you are not entitled to know the details. You need only know if there are any missing siblings. If you discover that you have a missing sibling, find out where in the family they belong. While you are asking, you might also inquire if either parent had any known missing siblings (your aunts or uncles). If any are discovered, you may want to make a small place for them in your house. Even a pretty plant, a small tree in the yard, or a pretty shell or stone set ritually in a special place may hold the place for the missing one.

Pay attention to your own children to make sure they have not taken on some of the missing child's fate. We should watch for unexplained sadness or depression in our children or any talk of death or longing for an unknown something.

Exercise 1
The Sibling Line

This exercise should be done for all of your siblings. When you have created the small representation of your sibling line, be sure to imagine standing in your place with them and taking all they can offer you in terms of energy and strength.

1. Create a special alter or place on a shelf or somewhere in your home to set up your "sibling line".

2. Using pretty stones, beads, or other special items, name one object for each of your siblings. If there is a missing sibling, be sure to include him or her as well as yourself. Place all of the objects in the right order (oldest first) from left to right.

3. If one of the siblings was missing, you may say the following ritual sentence to that sibling.

"Dear brother/sister, you are not alive and I am. I have missed knowing you, but from now on I will show you all the beautiful wonders of the world through my eyes. You have a place beside me."

Let the words come from your own soul. There is no need to apologize. You are innocent of any consequences for this fate and apologizing takes the dignity of the fate he or she has suffered away. It is not your business. If there is grief, consider that the grief is just love and let it flow out from you until the grief disappears and only the love remains.

Former Partners and Affairs

Sometimes what appears to be an intact sibling line is, in reality, not intact. One or more partners may have been involved with another in or out of the marriage and a child conceived and birthed. These hidden siblings are often kept a secret. Perhaps she has been given up for adoption (common in the case of teen pregnancy) or is being raised by a single mom somewhere (conceived in an illicit love affair). Occasionally, the father may not even have been told that he fathered a child. We humans have many ways of covering the evidence or sweeping away the debris of our transgressions. Once again, this cannot be said enough, there is no judgment placed or moralizing within the realm of constellation work. We constantly seek the strongest health and balance of the system, and so must look bravely and clearly into the results of our actions or the actions of those who came before us.

Occasionally a child may be raised by a father who is not his biological father although neither the child nor the father is aware of the deception. I touched on this earlier but want to reiterate here. The soul knows. Even though they are not conscious of this, somewhere deep in the soul, both the acting father and the child sense that something is not right. What we've seen in the constellation work is that the result of this deception by a woman can cause profound confusion and even mental illness in the child. Sometimes, even the mother isn't sure which man fathered the child, and we've seen other cases where the mother is not the mother but really an aunt or grandmother. There can be many confusing switches that occur out of guilt or bad feelings. We think we can hide the secret and distorted actions, but the soul always knows the truth.

One woman I worked with suspected that her second child was not the child of her husband. The suspicion was like a cancer eating her from the inside out until she couldn't live with not knowing. In her case, she finally paid for a paternity test, discovered her suspicion was true. She then contacted the man who actually fathered the child. It took tremendous courage for this young woman to face the results of her actions and take these steps to make the truth visible. The truth we can live with and adjust to—the lie can harm both mother and child. She acted honorably—even though it was painful. Whenever possible, we need to clear up the confusion with confession—or paternity tests when necessary.

Be very, very cautious in constellation work if a facilitator suggests that a parent is not the parent based on information coming only from the constellation and not factual information. We cannot use the constellation as a paternity test. These suppositions can cause further confusion, and the facilitators should refrain from suggesting this. If, within the constellation, there is a question around parentage, we can simply say, "There is something profoundly confusing here, and I cannot go further without the information." I've seen constellation facilitators handle this both ways and I strongly prefer to interrupt rather than infer without the true facts.

There is no simple exercise that can be done to reveal the carefully kept secrets that many families hold. We can, however, examine family rumors and try to back them up with the facts when possible. This is especially important when there is a pattern in the family of mental illnesses such as schizophrenia or suicidal depressions in one or more members of the system. Even the best-kept secrets carry a heavy price to those who come after. We should be on the lookout for severe systemic entanglements in these cases.

There are also many missing children across the entire globe that came out of the wanderings of soldiers during the wars or other loosely-taken affairs of the young or old. Often we cannot begin to sort this without factual information. My suggestion is that if you have always felt a longing for some unknown thing or person, perhaps just consider that your soul knows who it longs for and simply acknowledge the longing. Choose a cloud in the sky or a branch on a tree and simply say to it, "I don't know who you are, but my soul does, and I see you now and give you a place with me." Oddly, I've met many people in my workshops who say, "I always thought I had an older brother somewhere." or something like this. If you have always had this wisp of a feeling, simply acknowledge the feeling and let your soul wrap itself around it.

Recently, my husband Milt was exploring the habit he has of always taking up space by leaving his things on a counter, tabletop, or extra chair. It's as if whenever we enter a space he begins almost instantly to mark a place. We know from his adoptive history that there are still many relatives lost to him. He decided to try a simple exercise. Whenever he had the urge to occupy space or to set something down he would say, "I remember you." The exercise was oddly emotional for him although we could not know who had been forgotten or excluded. The small messes began to clear themselves as he did this simple action.

All of the topics discussed in this section have to do with being a child in our family of origin. This holding of place within our system as a child (no matter our age) is similar to place-holding in the mathematical numbering of zeros on either side of a decimal point. Our math only works if each place is held. As we explore precedence or right placement we can begin to understand that one place holds even as a new system is formed. At life's end, we have moved from child, to sibling, to parent, to relative, to grandparent and eventually, to ancestor. The flow of life down the generations is not haphazard or random but moves like water through a series of locks or levees. It flows best when each place is firmly maintained.

Prior to my work with the constellation, I studied behavior patterns and how they have been wired into the brain using Neurolinguistic Programming (NLP). Here we assume that the person is an autonomous individual and that his or her brain wiring contains both the problem and the solution. This is a good position to work from until we encounter the powerful influences of the larger energetic connection to the family of origin.

Now my picture has changed—to take in the great reservoir high in the mountains, and the gates of mother and father. We can work like a dog to change thoughts and patterns, but if there is little or no water flowing down from above, we can't succeed in life. Constellation work can re-open that place where the water flows out of the reservoir and increase our energy so that we can make better progress with patterns and structures.

During the first couple years of my Tuesday group, which met for almost three years, I also noted that just increasing the flow of energy from the family of origin doesn't necessarily mean you will suddenly have effective life skills. Often entanglements have crippled our early development, and we

81

need to take strong measures to learn some new tricks and strategies. Oddly, as I scan all the technologies I've worked with for "getting a life" I find that simple modeling, the way a child models behavior, can be most effective in determining what skills and directions you want to acquire. Look to people whose lives you admire and use them as models.

Things to Consider

Sometimes an ongoing and unexplained sadness or depression can be an indicator that a sibling is unaccounted for. If you can do it in an honoring and compassionate way, ask your parents if there were any pregnancies that did not come to completion. In general, we are not entitled to muck about in the affairs of our parents, so do this only if you have noticed this low burner depression. If you discover that you have a missing sibling, repeat the exercise from the earlier topic.

Abortion

Abortion presents a different scenario than a child lost in miscarriage, childbirth, or early death. The aborted child was not lost but taken. Once again, we approach the client who has chosen to abort a child (or several children) without judgment or moral shading. However, it cannot simply be skipped over as if it has no effect on the deeper soul of the individual or his or her current relationships systems.

Many women and men have spent a lifetime convincing themselves that the abortion was necessary and they are now okay with the decision. This is not what I've seen in working with these clients. Very often the soul does not agree with the head and suffers deeply as a result of this action.

When there has been an abortion, I generally do not do a full constellation but simply choose a representative for the aborted child and the other parent--the client stands in as herself. If the client is a man, the same steps apply. We sit in a small circle on the floor and, keeping close contact with the child, accept the consequences of the action with ritual statements. Together, mother and father must really see that child and accept the consequences of their actions.

My first trainer said that in order for a woman to have an abortion, she must disconnect part of her own soul. Like pulling a spark plug from an engine, her soul now runs on a little less power. There also seems to be a relationship between the number of abortions a woman has had and her current ability to carry on a strong relationship with a male partner. It can seem as if the soul itself were saying, "I have now taken too much and am not entitled to more".

The act of aborting a child is not just a woman's concern. The aborted child also has a father—whether he was informed of the conception or not. We must consider that his soul was also tugged away by the loss of this child. If he was not told, the consequences of the action are magnified for the woman. He was not given any say in the fate of the child, and this is perceived as an injustice done to him by the woman. In the work done in a constellation workshop between such a man and a woman, the woman says to the man, "I carry the full weight of this action. I did you an injustice when I did not tell you."

Our strength and our energy increase when we carry the full weight of guilt and sadness for what we have done. The consequences belong to the parent or parents and the child is innocent of all. We cannot bring the child back but we can acknowledge the presence of the tiny soul that came to us and was refused, and we are strengthened when we take responsibility.

In one constellation I saw, a couple (both were present) had three living children and when they were set up, all three felt very uncomfortable in their places and were angry and filled with a sense of looking for something else. Further knowledge from the couple revealed that each had participated in one abortion and, as a couple, they had miscarried one child. We brought all three missing children into the sibling lineup and the three living children (representatives) felt great relief and happiness to have the others there. Each of the living children seemed to be connected to one of the missing ones.

We were later told that, while the constellation was going on, one of the sons several hundred miles away who had been left at home suddenly had the urge to clean the entire house from top to bottom—a totally uncommon behavior for him. We often hear interesting stories such as this from participants that raise the interesting question of how this work affects the larger system even across time and space.

There have been several occasions when I've worked with women who were forced by their parents to give up a child up for adoption or to have an abortion. In these instances, the weight of the consequences and guilt falls on the parents who forced the loss of the child. Even in the cases where the child was conceived in incest, the soul of the mother still suffers the loss of the child.

Things to Consider

The results of earlier abortions can't be undone. This healing can only occur deep within the soul. However, if this discussion moved you, try one of the following exercises. I recommend this exercise even if you have convinced yourself that you have "dealt" with the issue and are feeling okay with it; you may be surprised.

Exercise 1
Healing Exercises for Abortion Experiences

1. Place yourself in a quiet space, put on some pretty music, and allow your feelings to rise to the surface and talk to your missing child. You may even choose the gender that feels right. You may use an object to represent the child if it helps you feel connected.

2. Tell the child that you recognize now what your actions cost him—his very life—and that now you are willing to see him and to recognize the price he had to pay.

3. Let your soul form the words without making excuses or blaming someone else. Simply accept the action as it was with its severe consequences.

4. Tell the child, "I give you a place in my heart forever, dear child."

Exercise 2
Honoring the Lost One

1. Plant a small bush or buy a pretty flowering plant and place it where you can see it and honor the child that was taken.

2. The purpose of this exercise is not to beat yourself up or further the guilt, but to give the child a place in the world. Tell the child, "From here you can see the many beauties of the world and the changing seasons."

3. You only need to keep this plant for a little while and then let it go—imagine the tiny spirit returning to the greater realms and finding only peace and happiness.

Note: It is not advised that you tell your other children about the aborted child, but if you feel the need to, simply tell them you lost the child. It's not their business to know of these things and can burden them further to get over involved in mom or dad's business.

Chapter Four
Forming a New System

Couple Relationships

Modern culture has turned weddings into huge commercial affairs that tax the resources of the parents and the young couple alike. We are surrounded with social pressure to put on a good show rather than to have two people come together to make what is essentially a sacred pact.

The man says, "I bring to you the strength of my entire lineage which is many thousands of years old, and I stand here and ask you to join my lineage." The woman says, "I bring to you the strength of my entire lineage and I stand here and ask you to join my lineage with yours." And when the couple engages in sexual intercourse, the man asks the woman to risk her life to bear him a child. And the woman agrees. Hellinger once told me that we have lost touch with how profound the sexual act is—that it is an agreement in which a woman essentially risks her life. This may sound extreme, but few would argue that the birth of a child is nothing short of a miracle—especially if they have born that child or witnessed its birth. How is it then that we could diminish the sexual act to gutter status or party games?

When two people come together from separate systems and marry or form a couple, a new system begins and, from this new system, the very possibility of new life begins. This does not mean the former systems are cut off from but rather are enfolded into the new family.

The joining of two ancestral lines sometimes brings together very different worlds. Each person contains the ingredients of their family of origin, but these ingredients are now cooked together with the partner's. We bring to the new system our own ancestral line complete with entanglements, strengths and weakness, a long history and, sometimes, very different cultural experiences. This system is now something quite new and fresh in the world, filled with possibilities and also with challenges. This is perhaps the true "blended family."

In ancient dynasties and monarchies, this coming together of two systems was carefully planned—more a business negotiation than a marriage. This remains true in some cultures today. However, in modern American culture, this significant union is often not given any more thought than the purchase of a couch or a car. We open and close new systems like fast food restaurants—one day there, the next not. It seems to me our culture—especially the children—are now paying a heavy price for taking a spiritual act too lightly. When we bind ourselves to another person's system, it is irrevocable—especially when children are born of that union.

Our children are suffering in body, mind, and spirit. The more deeply I've studied everything from cultural systems to brain systems, the more frustrated and hopeless I feel. The big pictures of the world I can do little about—it is fate. It is my sincere hope that like my story, *Albert's Manuscript*, we are in the cusp of some large cultural and spiritual transformation. If I can't change the big picture, then I'm content to work in small ways with this book, or a single constellation, or touching the lives of my students and the young people I teach. It is enough. And you can help.

Recognize your great responsibility and treat it accordingly. As individuals, we need to grow to our full strength and to act with that strength. Choose your partner from that strength—and not from a childlike entanglement or one too many margaritas.

My daughter Nichol is a doula and a natural childbirth educator. Each time she attends a birth, she calls and reports to me the many ways she fought furiously for that baby's right to attach to mom and dad in the first vibrating, hot moments of life. I cannot express to you how amazed I am by this child I created, my own daughter. She stuns me. By being a baby warrior, she is helping a whole generation get the best start they possibly can. She is in the midst of the action while I deal with the consequences of those actions using representatives in the constellation field.

But we all have a part to play. The other topics presented below are aimed to help you focus on the strength of relationship and then later, on becoming a parent.

Things to Consider

Please take a moment to ask some honest questions of yourself. The couple relationship is too important to accept less than what you want. Understand that there is no judgment or moral measurement here. You simply want to discover whether an entanglement or inability to separate from the family of origin is causing your relationships to be less than what you want.

1. How many relationships have you had that were intimate and ongoing?

2. How many relationships have you had that were brief—the classic one night stand?

3. What is the longest relationship you have been in?

4. Have you had a short-term relationship that ended in the conception of a child?

5. Do you have children with multiple partners?

6. Do your relationships make you stronger or weaker?

7. If you were to list the five primary qualities you want in a relationship, what would they be?

8. Have you had a relationship that contained all five qualities?

9. What kind of relationships do your parents or siblings have?

Exercise 1
Constellating the New System

This exercise is designed to give you only a first picture of the new system that you have created with your partner. This constellation can be done with representative objects for you and your partner to see how the relationship looks, or you may add children, parent, and grandparents if you want to see more of the links and connections. However, begin with the couple first.

1. Choose two representative objects, one for you and one for your spouse or partner.

2. Center yourself and clear all old, tired thoughts. Let what you do be fresh and from your soul.

3. Now constellate the two objects and be sure you are clear which is which and where the "face" is pointing.

4. Once you have finished setting up the constellation, simply look at the picture it has created. Are the partners together or separate? Do you have any feelings or sensations about either one? You can place your fingers on each object to see if any new feelings or thoughts come in. Be very aware of any energy that indicates a movement away from the relationship or family.

5. If either partner has a pull outward, place a second object to represent what they may be going toward. You may not know this specifically, but you may get an idea as you work with the pieces.

6. If it feels necessary, add representatives for the children or parents of both partners. Be willing to simply look at what the picture tells you.

Note: You may not be able to actually resolve issues using this approach but it may give you fresh insight into what is happening in your new system. Additional information can sometimes be gained by simply changing the direction or placement of the representatives or adding such loose elements as a "common goal" to see if that changes the energy of the constellation. Experiment with the connections between the members of your system and seek the strongest position. You cannot do it wrong if you stay open.

Exercise 2
Clearing for Couples

This exercise was originally an article that appeared in other places. I decided to just include it here in full as one of the exercises.

Clearing for Couples
Say it early, say if often—
say it before it becomes impossible to say!

Most relationships crumble not under the weight of large events but under the rubble of the unspoken small things. Learning a good process for "clearing" the small rubble of day-to-day living prepares us to weather the larger events should they arise. Trust, intimacy, and growth flower when a space is prepared for this regular "clearing" of the small things. When Milt and I got married we discovered that both of our previous marriages had crumbled under just such a weight—the small things unspoken. Because we didn't say the small things, they would all explode out destructively in an emotionally loaded moment.

When we married, Milt and I agreed to accept three guidelines for our marriage:

1. Everything happens for a reason—there are no accidents.

2. There is no such thing as a "bad" (or unworthy) feeling.

3. We would keep no secrets (of thought or action).

No accidents, no bad feelings, no secrets. To check our progress on this we began to do a regular "Clearing Session" and to create a space for allowing information to flow in the relationship. The *signal* for the need for clearing is when one or the other of us is not feeling connected to the other. It is as if when things go unspoken, a balloon blows up between the two partners and rather than risk pricking the balloon and saying something wrong, both partners begin to drift away from one another. If there is no communication the balloon just gets bigger and the risk greater. So, the solution is to clear it before it becomes too big.

The only real parameter set for a good clearing session is that either partner can say anything they need to say. Often, when we are doing this, we even begin by saying, "This is hard for me to say, but . . . ." The underlying message in this is, "Be gentle with me. I am about to take a risk, and I need to feel safe with you."

Be aware of any "Yeah buts" in the clearing. If you say what needs to be said and the partner automatically says, "Yeah but . . . you did or said . . . ." then you know this is straying from the purpose of the clearing session. Score-keeping and "yeah buts" are not allowed. If these old, destructive measuring patterns are not allowed, then we need to develop healthier communication patterns that help both partners to grow and go forward.

The secondary goal of a clearing session is not just that the stuff get dumped but that it go somewhere different and lead toward a resolution. The common stance in relationships is, "I am unhappy and it's because of something YOU are doing or not doing." This is a dead end. The clearing session gives us an opportunity to explore many of the following hidden premises for a relationship. Here are just the ones that come to mind for me.

1.   What is my expectation of you? Is it a true or fair expectation?

2.   What is my expectation for myself? Is it a true or realistic expectation?

3.   In what ways am I making your business my business? Or vice versa.

4.   Am I feeling guilty or incomplete about something and shifting blame?

5.   Is what I just said to you somehow reflective of what I think of myself?

93

6. Is anybody in the family using "hostile humor"? This is something I don't allow in my family (unlike the Simpsons). We do not seek intimacy or resolve issues by "poking fun" or making digging comments at someone in the family. Everyone is allowed to be in the family without teasing, nasty humor etc. coming at them.

7. Is there a systems problem here we can recognize and redesign? For instance, if every night at supper chaos erupts, we can analyze the process of "bringing supper to the table" to determine if the system is messed up somehow. Perhaps the kids need a snack at 4:00 to waylay the hungries. Perhaps a crock-pot supper would save stress at suppertime. Perhaps Mom or Dad really need 15 minutes each of alone time prior to supper. Perhaps other tasks and chores are choking the suppertime traffic. All of these questions analyze the "system" instead of shouting blame and accusations at each other. Milt and I have discovered that fully 90% of relationship difficulties are really "systems" problems. We can pick apart the system without picking apart each other.

8. Finally, what of our communication difficulties relate to our systems of origin (old ways of being) and our own inner systems (Am I staying my right age or are there things triggering me to shrink?)

When we take the small problems and irritations that come up during the clearing session and look at them from the "bigger picture" we can perhaps begin to actually design solutions and new systems to make life go smoother.

When one of the partners says something that may be perceived as "hurtful", be willing to take it in, turn it over, think of it in all of the above ways and even sleep on it for a few days before responding..

A solid, trusting relationship makes it possible for us to risk new behaviors and to grow in other arenas. Taking the time

94

and energy necessary to do these small clearing sessions can yield a big reward for both partners. Old, stale energy is released and new energy can come in. The frequency or length of the clearing sessions depends upon how often your balloon of the unspoken blows up. Initially, you may need to do it daily or weekly. Eventually, a clearing session is needed only when the drifting signal comes.

Remember, the best gift we can give to our children is to show them intimacy and trust between two parents. Children thrive when the first priority in the family is the relationship of mom and dad.

Keeping Love Alive

It's an amazing and unfortunate fact that many of us with unresolved family issues leave the family of origin only to end up recreating a distorted replica of what we just left behind. We choose a husband or wife and discover, shortly, that we're living again with mom or dad.

Milton Erickson, an insightful and talented psychotherapist, recognized over and over that many of his patients' problems arose from a failure to separate from the family of origin. This failure to separate can occur in one of two ways—either when the parents are unable to release the child or when the child is unable to embrace adult life fully and retreats back to mom and dad. In both cases the pointer would indicate the presence of unexamined and unresolved systemic issues within the family.

Most of us desire a partner relationship that has strong adult elements of love, respect, mutual support, shared interests, and an intimate physical and sexual connection. This healthy relationship can't occur if we remain forever a child. Actual chronological age has nothing to do with our ability to form and maintain a relationship with a partner. I've seen people at every stage of adult life who are unable to find and maintain the kind of partnership that he or she most deeply desires.

In reality, there is no homeostasis in partner relationships. An energetically-charged couple is always changing, advancing, and dancing toward some new future. If they are lucky, they travel along together. The image I have is like two skaters on a frozen pond holding hands and spinning. At one point in time, one has the momentum and is pulling the other along, and at another point in time, they spin and the other is now pulling. Often I encounter couples where one partner will say that she is doing all the forward work and the other is stuck in a rut.

Change is a fluid thing. When one partner does something dramatic, like release an age-old entanglement from their family of origin, he needs to have patience and let the change flush through. It isn't fair to suddenly alter the rules and expect the other partner to agree instantly to the changes. We have a new skin holding our organs and bones together and we need time now to discover who is living in that skin.

96

When partners grow at different rates, the urge is to try tugging the other along—or threaten to leave. In times of change, it's better to focus on your own individual growth and expansion with only the slightest invitation to your partner to join you in this expansion time. Eventually, one may grow beyond the other, and if this happens, you may simply lift off like a hot air balloon that is unable to stop itself from releasing the familiar tethers.

I'm always suspicious, however, when a client says, "I'm growing so fast and he refuses to budge." It often becomes apparent that the partner with so much pride in his or her growth is often a lightweight—always seeking the elusive, following butterflies across a field while the partner who *doesn't budge* may be firmly grounded both in their soul and on earth. Also suspicious, is when one partner looks down at the other as if she is better, which suggests a possible systemic imbalance relating to parent-child relationships.

If you have truly outgrown your partner, your inner feeling about him or her should be filled with gratitude and respect, and a simple acknowledgement that it is no longer here for you. We should be able to look at them clearly and say, "I honor you now as my former partner. I take all the good things you've given to me, and I treasure them."

Unlike the generations of a family, marriage or partner relationships should be eye-to-eye or close to that. In families children are under (or after) the parents and grandparents but this is not so for partner relationships. In these we are equal except for the slight shift that Bert Hellinger speaks of when he wrote, "I believe that relationships between men and woman work best when the man has just a bit more weight than the woman." According to Hellinger, this follows something deeply archetypal, even tribal—when the man's strength is held in service to the woman's. I question whether the woman's movement has done a great disservice to the soul of the family in attempting too much equality.

Some have argued with this controversial statement, but rather than judge it on a social level, I have judged it on the level of soul. It appears to go against the feminist movement, but perhaps we need to take a heartfelt look at what has happened since the woman was pushed out of the house and into the workplace. I like the picture of a world where the primary focus of family life is on the care of the young. This is too often being left up to strangers. Again, our culture pays a price.

The future of the human race depends upon how the couple approaches the birthing and raising of children. During the past twenty years, most of my focus has been on the issue of how to build strong families. As I entered a period of extensive studies, I realized that the issue is not social, not psychological, not political—but biological. Growing a child is about growing a brain capable of making intricate and elegant connections with itself. Good solutions grow out of the neurological flexibility of the brain.

Strong, conscious couples produce strong, conscious children, and we need a lot of consciousness to navigate this new world in which we live. Children left unattended, set aside, criminalized, or drugged for being children is not a solution. In tribal societies, it was the role of the man to secure the safety of the mother and her child, and I abide by this tribal knowledge. It is not an issue of equality but rather the right order of life. Through doing extensive studies, I now realize that the issue is that we have children left unattended while both mom and dad are striving to bring home the bacon. The consequences are wide-reaching and severe. More and more children are drugged, incarcerated, lured into gangs, and otherwise marginalized in our society.

I went through my own period of wondering why I hadn't met my Prince, the guy that would take care of all my needs like a good father rather than a husband. Then I got *liberated* and decided I needed to do it all alone. Unfortunately, raising children alone and independently is a tough road. Now, I've made a wide loop and realize that this tribal approach to families is the only natural way.

A partner is not a child—and not a parent—but a partner. We must ask in this new age what best serves the children.

When you feel that you and your partner are not growing at the same rate, it might be wise to examine the current relationship in the light of this systemic thinking. Have you married a parent or are you expecting your partner to parent you?

Things to Consider

If you are a person who feels unsatisfied in couple relationships, I strongly recommend you look backward first into your own system of origin. Here are just a few potential systemic entanglements that may be at the root of things. Most of these have been discussed earlier.

- An incomplete bond or movement to mom or dad
- Gender confusion coming from a missing sibling or other member of the larger system
- Entanglement with an earlier member of the system of origin
- Loyalty to the parent—unable to be happily in a relationship if mom or dad were not
- An emotional identification with the missing partner of one parent
- Multiple abortions

Scan your family history. Stick with the facts and not the narratives or stories. Who has been excluded or pushed out? Who died early or was not allowed to be present? Give each person his or her proper place in a ritual manner and refrain from any and all judgment of earlier members of your system. This honoring must happen deep within you or it will not be effective. If healthy relationships still elude you, a constellation with a trained facilitator may make visible what has previously remained hidden.

The Soul Needs Some Time

Occasionally after a constellation or any period of personal inquiry, a person may discover that she has unwittingly married a parent based on some hidden family script of which she had not been aware. The person now sees clearly what she has carried—and why. As a result of this new clarity, she may also realize that her mate is not exactly what she had in mind.

For example, a woman who has followed an echo in the feminine line where the women treat the men with disdain and brutal authority finds that she has married a weak man. He, likewise, has followed the echo in his own system of men who have chosen powerful, bossy women. This is not an accident. Both partners have been carefully chosen and groomed and have accepted their roles. These roles will not immediately or automatically reverse themselves or shift because a constellation has been done.

When I went through a 12-step treatment program many years ago, my first husband and I were counseled to not make any major changes for a year. This is good advice in constellation work or any intensive self-examination program. The soul needs some time to adjust and shift appropriately to the new picture of the family of origin. Personal stores of energy previously being spent on the entanglements are now freely flowing again. This can be disconcerting, and we need time to sort and explore this newly energized self. This is doubly true when the partner has also been exploring, doing his own soul work with the family of origin.

For several years after my training I ran a weekly constellation group. This group gave me the advantage of observing people who had done a constellation over time. Unlike the drop-in quality of a workshop, many people came weekly for a year or more. During this time I noticed that some people, when they had done a constellation, experienced a new release of energy into their lives. Suddenly, they feel like they have a lot to make up for and are in a hurry to do so. Time seems precious, and they are restless and ready. At last, they can find out about life without seeing each movement through the eyes of a child.

I suggest caution. This period is a little like the college student leaving home for the first time.

100

Perhaps the appropriate mode for couples would be to engage in a new courting period. Pretend you are getting to know each other all over again. Recognize that many of the old established patterns in the marriage may have been not me—not you and should be released completely. You now have the rare opportunity to meet each other anew. Ask many questions; analyze personal desired outcomes, mutual goals, dreams and desires. Aim all discussion toward a future that is entirely fashioned on what you both want most.

Old patterns are difficult to break. It takes vigilance. There are two things that can be very helpful. One is to ignore your first, second, even your third response. This will most likely be a knee-jerk response based on old programming. Only when we get further out in the ripple of possible responses can we come up with new material. A second, and I would like to recommend this to the whole world, is to disengage in all forms of hostile humor. Teasing, jabbing, making fun of, and sarcasm are all the ingredients of hostile humor. Good, clear, clean communication cannot grow out of hidden, passive aggressive hostile humor.

Hostile humor is a sneaky little rat. It will creep in and eat away at the trust and good feelings we have for one another. Begin to notice the difference between hostile humor and a loving humor. There is a difference. Hostile humor masks the thing that really wants to be said—but that we lack the courage to say.

As a married couple, Milt and I have a simple commitment to one another to never let the little things get big between us. This is why we do a regular clearing as the earlier section outlined. These little things, if unresolved, are like individual bricks that erect a wall between even the most loving couples. Once the wall is built it is difficult to bring it down again. If we deal with each individual brick—the wall never gets built.

While clearing, we both agree to listen to what is said without judgment or recrimination. We are free to say all the little, stupid irritating things, the big, enormous things, the silly things, and they all come out and we deal with it. Usually, there is nothing even to deal with except to express the things on our minds. What generally happens is we dump out those first ten responses and then get to where we are communicating beyond the knee-jerk response.

Since Milt and I are not only husband and wife but partners in business, we began using another simple premise to work from. We examine all issues from the view of a systems problem—and not a people problem. For instance, if things are not getting mailed in a timely fashion, rather than drop into blame and guilt-shifting, we inspect our mailing systems. We usually find out that there is a glitch in the systems such as not enough supplies, or things in awkward places. We improve the system—and the problem disappears.

A family can do this by identifying systems that include everything from supper routines to where to place the dirty towels. When hang-ups in the daily flow of a family or between couples are treated in this way, it takes the heat out. There is no need for hostile humor or jabbing. We simply need to sleuth out the systems problem and take care of it.

Another example might be if suppertime is a nerve-wracking, emotional dart-throwing time in your household, consider looking at the whole supper period as a delivery system for supper. How could you improve the system? Where does it hang up? What are the glitches in the system? This actually makes the analysis fun and challenging and not a weapons arsenal for one person to attack another.

In my former marriage, nothing was ever fully cleared and so when some crises arose, all the unspoken things came crashing into the moment and we ended up hurting one another badly. This unhappy pattern damages relationships—and it damages families.

Now I encourage my students to say it all, say it often, say it anyway—before it gets so big you cannot say it at all.

Things to Consider

1. Allow plenty of time after constellation or serious inner work to let the soul and the systems settle down again. Give it this time!

2. Create your own clearing technique and use it often and with regularity, perhaps even daily until you get the hang of it. It is important to use the clearing as a common tool and not just a stop gap when things fall

totally apart. If you form the habit of clearing (and analyzing the system) it will serve you well when a serious issue arises. See earlier exercise.

3. Take time to analyze patterns and systems with each other, within the household and anyplace else there is a problem. In this way, no one is to blame except the poorly-constructed system.

4. Pay attention to the use of hostile humor around you. You will find it in the tone of voice or content, you will find it among your children, and you will find it common in others. Once you begin to recognize the difference between hostile humor and just plain fun, you can make small corrections. Hostile humor is a signal that some-thing needs to be cleared.

When Fate Intervenes in the Couple Relationship

Here is one final note before leaving the subject of couple relationships. Occasionally fate intervenes and one of the partners becomes disabled or ill. Suddenly the balance of give and take is irrevocably tipped. Now one of the partners must do more for the other without expectation of return. This rests in the hand of fate, and we can do nothing but take our role now as caregiver and do so with full understanding that we now give and do not take. Likewise, the disabled partner is now forced to take without the return movement of giving. I once worked with a woman who was married to an elderly man who had become unable to return what she needed in the relationship. This woman's loving attention to her disabled partner was remarkable. She honored him, cared for him, and still was able to begin fashioning the next phase of her life. When he passed away a few years later, she was able to move forward without guilt.

If you find yourself in this situation, realize that you must also increase your ability to take from others more freely and, in this way, maintain a balance for yourself. Do not become a martyr. That will serve no one. Fate has taken a hand in your life, and for a time, you must bow to it.

If you are the person who has become somehow disabled, the same is true. You must recognize that fate has dealt you a hand in which you must take—and not give back. If you carry this burden without blame or anger, you will gain strength even when you have lost it.

Things to Consider

If your partner or spouse has become unable to participate fully in the relationship, be careful not to let your children step into the breach. It will be very important for you to find the adult support necessary to allow you to take care of your emotional needs. This can come from family, friends, or adult support groups. Take care to find a healthy one. During times of crises or extended illness, pay special attention to your own rest, food, and support.

Chapter Five
Becoming Parents

Entering a New Stage of Life

Becoming a parent is a mile marker in life. It signals the true end of childhood and the significant undertaking of starting a new generation of human beings in the world—or a new system. Responsibilities pile up, finances grow tight, and personal needs suddenly take a back seat. We shift position from being the center of our parents' world to the peripheral edge of our own newly forming world. It's easy to lose our place.

In an ideal world we would have been fully prepared for the task by our elders. Many tribal cultures still include ancient rite of passage rituals intended only to prepare the young for adulthood. Many things unfold during this time. The youth is very often taken from the mother and separated. The community rallies around the youth to give all that is needed. When the rite or ritual is complete, the child is now acknowledged publicly and ceremonially as a man or woman.

I explore this potent time in a previous book, *The Lonely Place, Revisioning Adolescence and the Rite of Passage*, and rather than stray into that topic, we'll simply take note that modern culture often does a poor job of initiating young people into the task of parenting. Just as we made a passage from the spirit world into our family of origin at the moment of conception, now we take another spiritual journey into the realm of being a parent. Unfortunately, children become like cotton balls and begin to absorb all the unfinished business of the parents.

When my first child was born, I was torn between staying with her and continuing to work. My solution was to open a day care center. I bought an old church, renovated it, and started The Red Apple Day Care Center. After many months of taking care of a gaggle of small children, I began noticing that the children tended to reflect whatever my mood was that day. If I was unhappy and uptight, we all had a rough day. When I was balanced and feeling good, we had a great day. In essence, I had to take good care of myself before I could take care of the children.

Children are content when mom and dad are taking care of themselves and their relationship. I'd like to write that about four more times so it has a chance to sink in. When the couple is strong, the children feel safe. There is nothing to absorb or take on for mom and dad.

When early development is incomplete or I am still entangled, a part of me remains hanging out in childhood and putting my relationship first is difficult. I am unfinished. In an attempt to finish myself, I may be over focused on my children—determined to do it right. If my partner is also unfinished (likely he is), then this puts a lot of pressure on the child. He is suddenly the center point for the whole new system—around him all else revolves.

When children must *be* something for the parents—besides a child—they lose their place. When adults use a child to complete their own development, they have lost the place of parents, and the family is now out of order.

Everywhere I go, I see evidence of this dynamic operating such as children bossing their parents around, making demands, acting terribly. When I see small children acting this way in a store or public place, I wonder if their small souls are protesting the weight that has been placed upon them. Think about it. Mom and dad's entire happiness suddenly depends upon if the child is good and smart—or not. Perhaps tantrums and acting out is the child's soul saying, "We are out of order here."

Parents are Parents with a capital 'P.' They are the boss, the big one, the one who knows, the one who understands—the one who insures survival. We must keep our place with our children or a deep fear and insecurity arises within them.

Growing Ourselves up First

When we have unresolved issues of our own, the scenes play out one by one with our own issues at the forefront. For instance, suppose I think that my parents didn't support me enough, or were too critical. As a result of this, I follow my own child around with small gold stars and smiles and oh-so-nice words of praise until the child thinks that even what he puts in his diaper has true merit—simply because it came from his precious little body. This behavior makes a child too big in the right order of the family. And unfortunately, it also doesn't fill in what I may have missed in my own development. Instead I end up with an overindulged child who thinks he is entitled to anything and everything.

For instance, I worked with a client, an adult male, who had struggled with fear and shyness most of his life. He now had a four-year-old son that he says, "Is just like me." Because of his own history, he was desperately trying to make his son less afraid. As far as I could tell, his son was simply passing through normal childhood stages (fear of monsters in basements, etc.). As parents, we lose perspective and fear our children will tumble into the same pain we experienced as children. However, the best approach is to take care of our own historical patterns and not attempt to do it through our children.

We return again to the Orders of Love. Young members of a system are not entitled to carry the fate of a previous or earlier member. This is a significant statement. It's also a freeing statement. Although it's painful sometimes to watch those who came before us (parents or relatives) struggle with alcoholism, depression, or other unhappy patterns, there is a liberating relief in knowing that we didn't cause it, and we can't cure it for them. It is their own fate, and they must carry it.

Becoming a parent is an opportunity to stop the trans-generational flood of issues. It is our chance to say, "The buck stops here." Parenting is a difficult enough task without allowing the past to flood the present and land on our children. In a sense, we are a wedge between the generations and can stop this from happening. Stand in your place as parent to your child. Do not allow him to become partner or friend or parent to you. He is the child. As unnatural as it sounds, I love to hear a parent answer a child's incessant "Why?" with "Because I said so, and I am the mom." This statement clearly draws the lines between generations.

I worked with a single mother who was trying to get along with a sixteen-year-old daughter. In the constellation it became clear that the daughter had played many roles. She had been partner, friend, and sister to her mother. The end result was that she also became judge and jury and constantly criticized her mother. In this instance, both mother and daughter had lost their places and were unhappy with the fuzzy arrangement. When the generational lines are blurred, it becomes difficult for the natural separation of the older child to occur. The child has too many hats to wear. How can she leave her mother all alone?

Keeping the Balance of Give and Take with Children

All relationships—family, business, and otherwise—are in a constant state of balancing. We may not be conscious of this measuring of each moment but it exists. How much is given and how much is taken is always being weighed. Although this is different from an entanglement or carrying another's fate, it's an important concept to grasp and monitor within the family sphere.

Infants and very young children are not as subject to the balance of give and take. They just naturally take—or they wouldn't survive. In essence, parents give, children take. This is the right arrangement in the downward flow of life. The first thing children take is the very gift of life itself from the parents. Then, as they grow, they take all they need for survival without giving back anything of substance. For this reason, children forever owe the parents for this gift, and it cannot be balanced—it can only be paid forward to the next generation.

However, parents and children need to be aware of the constant balancing of family life. Even a two-year-old is able to measure when he has taken too much—or been deprived of something necessary. Brothers and sisters constantly balance things out between themselves—a kind of "eye for an eye" justice. Children are naturally greedy, but part of this greediness is a continual test to see where they belong and how much they can take. This is where the chore of parenting becomes an art form.

I struggle to say this in a good way. When we give children too much, we burden them. Remember, we have given them life—already the debt is so large—and when we give and give we kick the balance out of whack. Paradoxically, when the balance has been tipped, the children will angrily beg and beg for more. This is a signal that we have given them too much.

For instance, a weekly allowance can be taken more graciously when the correct numbers of chores have been done and the allowance has been earned. Or we can buy a car for an adolescent child, but the balance is best maintained when the youth is required to invest something of himself into the car. My children attended high school in an affluent area. Over and over I saw parents purchase brand new cars for their children without asking anything back—and the car ends up smashed against a tree three weeks later. It is as if the soul of the young person knows they don't deserve this much and so they cannot take it freely.

Children buried in a great abundance of toys, and stuff, or later clothes, electronics, phones, and designer this and that become disturbed deep within because some part of them recognizes that they take too much and can give nothing back to restore the balance. Naturally, the child can't or won't tell you of this disturbance because it's out of visible awareness. Even praise and good wishes for your child can backfire. Instead of raising their self-esteem, it inflates it unnaturally when the child doesn't feel as though he has earned the praise. Empty compliments insult the soul. The soul knows when it deserves to be complimented or praised.

My son once spent an entire evening creating a truck out of small tubes of rolled paper. With complete focus he worked with a hot glue gun and tape, using all his wits to get it to drive. His investment in the truck was considerable. When his teacher placed it in a showcase at school, he came home really pleased that his efforts had been noticed. This felt to me like a nice balance between what he had given to the project and what he had received. However, the special notice may not have been necessary. When a child is creatively engaged in a project, the task becomes its own reward. Any later attention is just frosting.

This is a parenting goal—to encourage your child to become fully engaged in his or her own creative process—and to let that be its own reward. If we make them dependent on the treat, or the praise, or a ribbon we rob them of this important motivational strategy.

We are not bad parents if we close our palms occasionally (often?) and say no.

Let go of unnecessary parental guilt. It is an indulgence we can't afford. Someone once told me (a wise someone) that if you are feeling guilty, look around, someone is manipulating you. There is a great deal of pressure in our society to satisfy needs that are really only wants disguised. I read an interesting article that said we have moved in our economy from *satisfying* needs to *creating* them. This seemed very true to me at the time. I see many parents who give so much stuff—but fail to satisfy real needs.

Balancing the Give and Take with Couples

The balancing of give and take is important in all relationships. If we could analyze small transactions between partners, we would find that the operating dynamic is who gave what, how much, and when. We can't seem to help ourselves. We measure these things—we do. When Milt gets up off the couch to get me a glass of water, the tiniest debt is incurred. When I see him sneezing and I get up to grab the box of tissues for him, the debt is now paid.

It sounds so simple, but when you compound this over hundreds and hundreds of interactions we have with our partner over time, the balance can quickly tip toward the negative. Soon we are score-keeping.

Hellinger once said in a workshop that we should give back to our partner what was given—and a little bit more. If we have this flowing in a positive way (and not scorekeeping) our relationship will flourish.

In the same vein, Hellinger said when somebody does something against the partner relationship, we should give back as good as we got. When I read this, I laughed aloud. In my first marriage I was such a saint—forgiving again and again—and that marriage failed.

Forgiving should be left to the saints—it's not for ordinary mortals. When an injustice (or a nice deed) is done to us, we never really forget. Better to just give it back in kind and be done with it.

For instance, if a man cheats on a woman in a marriage, should she just *forgive* him and go on? According to Hellinger, this is a sure way to end the relationship. If the balancing mechanism is not allowed to operate, then all the weight of the action falls on the perpetrator and there is no relief. Rather the wife should say to him, "Oh buddy, you are going to pay good for this one." Then carry through somehow to make him pay for what he has done—a trip to Greece for instance.

This is true not just in the big events, but in all the small, daily transactions. When we do too much for anybody without accepting something back, it actually burdens the relationship.

Relationships that succeed are constantly balancing between giving and receiving more, and a little more, and a little more. Unfortunately, many of us get caught in a reverse balancing by countering small wounds with additional wounds (perhaps a little larger) until the relationship is "balancing" straight into oblivion.

Being a couple requires great energy and perseverance. We stand beside another person and do what is necessary to strengthen each other. We have a greater chance for success if we monitor this giving and taking, if we do daily or weekly clearing of all the small grievances, and if we enter a wonderful balancing movement of kindness for kindness and not cut for cut.

And when the couple is strong—the children will thrive.

Things to Consider

1. Do your own work first. This does not mean spending years in therapy, but scanning your life for results. Are you going where you want to be going? Do you feel free to design the life you most desire? Do you feel you have your full energy without experiencing a lot of depression, frustration, or patterns that halt all activity when you have nearly reached the mark? A great sage once said, "The only thing you can give to others is your own state."

2. Are you a model for your children, showing them that life can be rich and full and that you are a life-long learner? Do you take healthy risks to gain new ground? Are you able to self-regulate frustration, anger, and sadness? Do you have chronic patterns, either emotional or physical, that keep you from moving forward? Do you sometimes not feel your right age but feel stuck in elementary school or adolescence or some other life stage? All of these can be signs of developmental gaps or entanglements.

Constellation work can help release you from the family of origin, and can help your children move forward. However, there are many steps you can take without a constellation. What is remarkable about human beings is that we develop patterns, and there

112

are not as many patterns operating as we may first think. What is also remarkable is that these patterns can occupy so much of our energy and life. Negative patterns are a signal to the self that something is stuck. Notice your patterns and ask, "What do they mean about me.

3. Make sure your child does not take on burdens from earlier members of the family or from the loss of a sibling. Entanglements are not always visible. In fact, more often they remain hidden or invisible. One way to recognize when we are entangled is when there is no logical reason for reoccurring patterns of sadness, fits of anger, moods that won't break, or tendency to self-destruct. Children are very, very willing to take on and carry the burdens of the family. Just as we watch their diets and other healthy patterns, we must watch for entanglements.

4. One of the simplest ways to prevent children from taking on your own emotions is to simply tell them not to carry anything for you. "This sadness is mine, dear, you needn't take it on. I am the parent here, and I will deal with it. This belongs to me, not you. I am the parent—you are the child." These little reminders, when done well (without anger) serve to keep the child from stepping out of place.

5. Constantly monitor the balance of give and take between family members. This balance is a finely-tuned instrument in any family. Remember that even at a very young age children can be required to "give back." Do not do everything for them. You gave them life—that is already a debt they cannot repay. Likewise, they can give to each other but generally the flow is from oldest down to youngest. If you see a younger child trying to give to everybody in the family, this child may be entangled in some business that is not his or her own.

113

6. Remind your child that you are the parent and he is the child. This can never be changed. Children also feel these ancient orders of love, so when you reassure them of that order, they feel safer. Children may step out of place and try to parent you, or become identified with some earlier member of the system. They need to be reminded what is theirs, and what belongs to others.

7. Keep the children in their right place. If a child is critical and judgmental of any parent, simply explain to them that they are not in any way entitled to judge the actions of the parent. However, use good judgment. If there is abuse in the family, safety comes ·first. When we hear a lot of mouthy and abusive language toward the parent, it may be another sign of entanglement.

8. Take special care during a divorce or separation. If there has been a divorce, do all that is possible to make sure the child is connected physically and/or emotionally with both parents without forcing a split of his or her loyalties. When physical connection is not possible, speak well of the other parent. This way you support the part of the child that comes from that parent. Again, deal with whatever issues you may have left over from the dissolved union.

Note—if you do have a child who seems unnaturally sad, angry, or confused recognize that this child may be carrying something heavy within the system. I strongly recommend you attend a constellation workshop and set up this child to see with whom he or she may be connected. Although this is a self-help manual designed to assist you in managing your family system from afar, sometimes a constellation is the best route to take. It is most useful in revealing the hidden dynamics of our system and could prevent a life of hurt, anger, or even suicide. However, be careful in selecting a facilitator. Do your homework and ask around.

Exercise 1
Monitoring the Family Balance

1. Practice using the clearing technique on a daily or weekly basis as needed. You are doing this not just to clear grievances, but to co-create the relationship you both desire. When the air is cleared we can be more creative in finding solutions to the many irritating issues that arise every day. We can even keep the romance alive.

2. Monitor the balance of give and take between you and your mate. Do you score keep? When was the last time you caught your partner doing something right and offered a compliment? When was the last time you tipped the balance of give and take in a positive direction? Begin doing small kindnesses for your partner. Notice the change.

3. Notice and REMOVE any hostile humor. Do not tell stories at his expense, and do not point out small flaws or tease your partner. Begin to discover true humor between you—the times when you can laugh together about something that happens. Snide, childish digs make it very difficult for both adult partners to stay adult. When one reverts to playground behavior, the temptation is to follow.

4. Keep the couple business out of earshot of the children.
You and your partner are adults and must deal with life's issues between you. Do not make a child your confidant—it is not their business and burdens them.

5. Honor any former partners of your mate. In some way, the failure of the first relationship brought the new partner to you. This is a gift, and if you honor that gift, the new relationship will thrive more easily.

6. Be nice, but be straight. There is nothing more dangerous than the unspoken.

Exercise 2
Things to Consider For Parents with Their Children

The daily interactions with children are so ongoing and continuous that the following exercises are more suggestions and guidelines. Do practice them daily.

1. Allow your children to solve their own problems at a very early age with as little assistance as possible. It grows a dynamic brain!

2. Keep your business as a parent separate from their business as a child. This includes family finances, couple issues, etc.

3. Recognize and encourage the child's urge to separate. We still need boundaries and rules—but we need to let the child make mistakes in order to grow.

4. Teach children the difference between hostile humor and just plain fun. Hostile humor hurts—happy humor makes people genuinely laugh.

5. Encourage engagement with the creative process to be its own reward. Do not drown your child in praise or stuff. Allow them to earn small items with their own engaged activities. This will help maintain the balance.

6. When your child becomes a teen, do not automatically buy him a car—or hand over a trip or even a college education. When they must earn all or part, it allows them to take ownership and also keeps the balance. See this as their initiation toward becoming an adult.

7. Please pay careful attention to a child who appears to be overly burdened for his or her age and circumstances. This child may be entangled with a

previous member of the family and need special attention or a constellation.

Exercise 3
Monitoring Strength in the Family

To do an energetic check up on the strength of the family and the children, you may once again use the small objects as representatives. Your goal is only to get a clearer view of family dynamics and not to make any assumptions about how your children are doing. Although a similar exercise was presented earlier as a "first check" on the new system, it is a good idea to repeat it here after learning more about the balance of give and take.

1. Choose objects to represent yourself, the other parent, and all children including any missing or miscarried ones.

2. Clear a space on the floor or table and designate this as the *knowing field*.

3. Center your own inner energy with a few deep breaths or do a couple of slow stretches.

4. Pick up the objects one at a time in any order but be sure that you know which child or adult the object is representing and which part of the object is forward facing.

5. Now move all the objects one by one into a constellation.

6. Stand back and generally see how that picture feels for you. If you want a better reading on any single person, simply place your fingers on them and see what you can feel.

7. Notice in particular if any one person within the constellation seems to be isolated or turned away or otherwise feels distant from the rest of the family.

8. If your energy feels very clear, see if you can find the strongest order for the family. Place the children in order from oldest (left) to youngest, and then place you and the other parent in front of them. Now see how it looks to you.

Again, this tabletop constellation is not likely to resolve issues but it can reveal them—or begin to.

Childlessness—By Choice or Fate

Here we take a special bow to those who, either by fate or choice, do not have children. Becoming a parent is the natural order for most human beings. Those who elect to be in non-traditional relationships, who have medical complications and cannot conceive, or who have simply not married or selected a partner fall into a different order. Some people simply opt out of becoming parents for reasons of their own. In all of these instances I cannot presume to know or even suggest what is true for any one person. Perhaps the best recommendation is to simply accept what is and to bow to the fate as it is.

When we try to force fate or change fate, we enter into a gray zone where the natural orders may become disturbed. For instance, when a childless woman finds her barrenness so painful that she seeks a solution by adopting another woman's child, she may find that the adopted child cannot fill the empty womb. Or when two homosexuals go to extraordinary measures to have a child together, and the natural mix of mom and dad is changed to something else, they may find the disorder difficult to overcome. Or when a sperm donor suddenly finds himself wondering about his role as 'father' to countless unknown children . . . .

Other than adoption, I've not seen enough of these circumstances within the constellation to speak effectively about the observed results. I will stand with Hellinger's observation that it is always best when we bow to our fate and acknowledge what is. He does, however suggest that childless couples can fulfill their *fruitfulness* in another way, for instance by offering their work with a deep sense of service to the future generations, or by creating something that is life-giving in its own way.

Milt and I have no children between us, and at times this has made me sad. But as I look back now, I can see that we turned this procreative urge into a creative urge, pure and simple. Our common children are the seventy-plus documentaries that we produced for public radio. This can be a solution for childless couples—to create a "common child" in projects or work that must be conceived, nourished, and brought forward into the world to serve the world.

121

Fate is sometimes a difficult master. As I've studied the work of Bert Hellinger and others who look at life through a lens of reality, I can see that true strength comes from accepting and "acknowledging what is." I meet many people who struggle with being alone, being childless, having deep disappointments with the fate they have been dealt. Life really does work in mysterious ways, and I have no simple answers, no panacea or magic bullet that can make it better. I do know that when we turn more deeply inward, life can sometimes take another turn. When we accept our fate humbly—and with courage—we are made stronger by that fate.

The Overmedication of Children

Before I leave this topic of parenting, I want to caution my readers against the overuse of psychotropic drugs to medicate a child's symptoms. Emotions and behaviors are primary indicators of what needs tending both within the emotional world of the child and in the larger system around him. We need those indicators to discover how to fix whatever has gone out of order. Imagine a newborn infant who could not cry or fuss as a way to let you know what is going on?

I fear we are in danger of placing the burdens of our society's problems on the slender shoulders of our children. For example, when our classrooms fail, we blame the child and diagnose them as Attention Deficit Disordered or "hyperactive." Or when our marriage fails, we diagnose the child as depressed or bipolar and put him on drugs. Or when the food supply fails to nourish, and the television or computers have taken over their minds, we call them fat and lazy. Or when our economic systems fail and parents are forced to hold multiple jobs—and our children go crazy—we diagnose the child as disordered.

This is social madness. Children are growing bodies, brains, and young spirits. They should be free to develop with as little interference from us as possible. I realize that we have been trained to trust the doctors and the diagnosis, but I don't. Designer drugs are rapidly coming into being merely to fatten the pockets of the drug industry. The creator gives us such things as sadness, anger, stress, and even physical symptoms to tell us where we need to go. If the signals are fogged by drugs, then we are simply—in the fog.

Chapter Six
Fate and the Family of Origin

When Stuff Happens

Not every family is fortunate enough, especially in this modern age, to stay intact with mother, father, and the children all remaining in the same household and sharing each other's fate. There are many circumstances that can interrupt or shatter this single unit and give it many different configurations. A parent dies, the partners divorce and choose new partners, a sibling dies, or the siblings of one family are asked to blend with the siblings of another family. Members of a family can suffer catastrophic illness, early death, severe substance abuse and mental illness.

There are instances in which a couple cannot handle the birth of a child and an adoption or social services intervention splits up the family unit. There are also large social or cultural movements such as war and immigration that can affect multiple generations of a family. The possibilities are endless, and each shift or change in the structure should be taken seriously, with deep understanding of the consequences of the actions undertaken.

Whenever a man and a woman come together and even the possibility of a child being conceived is present, a deep bond is formed within their souls. We may not acknowledge it socially or culturally—or even know about it—but the bond is there. When a child is conceived, the consequences are even greater.

The shifting structures of a family can best be managed by honoring the orders of love and paying particular attention to the layers of loyalty and precedence that exist within the larger soul of the family and to the hidden orders of love. My experience with this work shows me that the soul maintains its loyalty to the biological family even when that structure is shifting. Each of us has the right to belong to the two legs of our ancestral line; it's as if nature dictates it. Below are separate discussions of different acts of fate or the consequences of

125

events that we may be confronted with, and some suggestions on how to deal with them in a loving way.

Divorce and the Myth of the Blended Family

When my first husband and I divorced, he married a woman with two children similar in ages to our three. We had an agreement that the kids would live six months with him and six months with me. We all had illusions that we were mature and responsible adults capable of blending these two families. It's interesting to see what happens when you toss two first born siblings together into the same household. With the powerful, controlling, energy of first position, a war can ensue. There was no blending—only collision.

Today's families are hugely complex. We often have multiple marriages or partners, children from different fathers living as one family unit, and every possible combination that can be configured. In one family I worked with, circumstances were such that the stepparent was given custody of a child and then remarried. This child was no longer living with *either* biological parent.

Blood ties are powerful. Many people want to minimize this significant biological factor—to the detriment of their own family systems and the lives of the children. Sometimes, we justify our own inability to hold and maintain the marriage by pointing to one partner and saying "bad person." Even as I write this I can hear many of you slide into this way of justifying. "But he was bad. He treated me badly and the kids badly and is/was a bad person."

Unfortunately, there are bad parents and partners. Burdened beyond their capacity to deal, they take it out on all around them. However, the biological bond seems to transcend the physical and exist on a soul level. A child longs for his or her parents. Period. We may be capable of stacking piles of stories and rationalizations on this simple fact, but this bond still resides there deep within the soul. If we have full awareness of this powerful soul bond we can, with extreme caution, navigate the uncertain waters of the blended family.

There is no ideal solution for combining siblings from two families into one household. Perhaps it is most useful to encourage and give full permission for separate—but together. The families remain separate although they live together. Part of the problem is that the only true stepparent comes about when the previous partner dies and the new one "steps in" to fill his or her place. If the true parent is still alive, the new partner is simply that—a new partner to mom or dad. A stepparent who tries to replace a biological parent will find him or herself in a bind.

When a man and a woman conceive a child, a new system springs into being naturally with all the links and connections built in. This is not true when two separate systems come together by marriage only. In truth, the new system is a contract between only the two partners and no amount of cajoling can blend the two separate systems. Even when the new partners have a common child, they essentially form another new system. It gets very complicated, these hidden orders of love, but I believe they can be negotiated in a way that allows each system to flourish.

For example, when we first began to learn this way of thinking, my current husband Milt stopped trying to be a father to my children and even began to say to them, "I'm only your mother's husband." There was an immediate release of the tension in our house. Suddenly he didn't have to be something he wasn't, and the children didn't feel forced to accept him as anything but my partner. Of course, this does not mean that all involved will not come to care about and respect or even love one another. Rather, the caring can evolve naturally when there is no pressure to be a parent to a child who is not biologically yours.

The partner who comes into a pre-existing system with children will do well to recognize that the bond of a parent with his or her children is stronger than the bond with the new partner. In essence, the new partner cannot compete with the kids. If competition comes into play, havoc will ensue. I remember telling Milt one time, "If you force me to choose between my children and you—you will lose!" He got it.

The orders of precedence in blended families need to be observed and respected if the new system is to succeed. For instance, my former husband, with whom I had three children, actually holds precedence to my new husband, Milt. This has nothing to do with how much I love and cherish my new husband. This has to do with the subtle ties that bond us with others. Wayne and the children came first in my life, and therefore hold precedence in the natural order of my life.

128

The newly-formed system can thrive when former partners are given their place with honor and respect. This cannot be emphasized enough. It's extremely destructive to cement the new relationship by constantly badmouthing the former husband or wife. It damages the new couple, and it is especially damaging to any existing children. I experienced this personally with my son, as mentioned earlier. When I recognized my divisive attitude toward his father, I began immediately to undo the damage with subtle comments such as, "I am glad that you got your father's head with numbers and not mine." Or, "You're getting so tall and handsome—just like your father."

It's deeply relieving to the soul of the child to hear that they are like the other parent—and that you approve. The shift in my son was immediate and enduring. He no longer had to worry that if he became like his father, perhaps I would divorce him also.

When one parent constantly criticizes the other parent, it sets up a profound confusion in the soul of the child who loves both parents equally. Again, this love is a deep bond in the soul and not dependent on the actions of either parent. It is even possible not to like a parent and still this deep flowing love exists.

Allowing my son to make a movement toward his father had more lasting consequences than I could have realized at the time. Thomas spent three years working on construction sites with his father and in the company of men. Sadly, in the fall of 2002, his father was killed in a small plane crash. Since that terrible day, I've been deeply grateful that the new understanding I gained from this work gave me freedom from my old anger—and that my son was able to have that rich time with his father without my interference.

Except in rare cases of neurological or physical disorder, children are not born angry, sad, or fearful. These behaviors or emotions in children signal that something is not in order. Issues have not been resolved in the family of origin, the previous marriage, or something is amiss in the current marriage. Angry children are not normal. Something is up with them.

Likewise, angry parents are not normal. Something is up with them.

Let me use an example from one of my clients whom I will call Carrie. Carrie is an adult woman with three children and a fairly solid marriage that she wants to continue. However, she experiences intense periods of rage that she feels are hurtful both to her marriage and to her children. She can't seem to control these rages despite her best efforts to change. Two of her children are from a previous marriage (father not present), and a third child was aborted (fathered by her current husband). They have one living child between them.

Already we feel the complexity of systemic issues within her current system. When we scan her family of origin, we find that Carrie's father also reacted with rage and extreme criticism of Carrie's mother. They divorced when Carrie was twelve. With further inquiry, we find that Carrie discovered just a few years ago that her mother fell in love with a boy when she was sixteen, got pregnant, and was forced by the families to give the child up for adoption. To add to the systemic mix, Carrie's father also had younger twin sisters that were stillborn. Are your eyes crossing yet? Mine certainly do when we begin to unscramble how time and events have so thoroughly scrambled some families. Even with all these many issues on the table, we still can't be certain which systemic factors (if any) may be contributing to Carrie's current problem of episodic rage. In fact, her story is more typical than atypical.

In her constellation, we discover that the 'traveling' rage was perhaps first formed when Carrie's mom was forced to abandon both her lover and her child. The new husband cannot compete with such ties on her heart, and so spends twelve or more years feeling left out. He reacts with anger. In this case, when the missing baby brother and its father (her mother's early love) are given a place in Carrie's life, the rage dissipates immediately. She actually grins ear to ear in the session and is completely mystified at how good she feels.

In systemic terms, we would say that Carrie was *identified* with the missing ones. As long as they were tossed out, she would continue to toss herself out. I do not mean to simplify such complex energetic connections, but you can see how intricate they become, and why the constellation is such a useful tool to untangle the entangled.

The action of two people loving and conceiving a child is an action outside the moral boundaries of any society. No matter the rules, the bond has been formed and is irrevocable. To think that such mistakes can simply be swept under the rug and made to disappear causes systemic problems that begin echoing down through a system.

Carrie may still have to work further by looking at the child that she also abandoned when she aborted her third child. Unfortunately, we live in a society that attempts to minimize the consequences of such actions as aborting or giving up a child, divorcing or separating children from parents. We somehow think that there are no consequences if the problem is somehow made to go away. It doesn't go away. One of the key "orders of love" is that every member of a system who rightfully belongs must be given a place. Exclusion—or removal—causes disorder.

Divorce and remarriage are painful enough for the children without asking the child, in subtle ways, to choose one parent over the other. This split is too awful for them. Children must be allowed to move freely, both emotionally and, if possible, physically between both mother and father. In order for a child to drink from both cups—mother and father, as we explored earlier—he or she must be free to move from one to the other.

This is sometimes difficult. In the case of a woman named Sarah, her former husband and the father of her children was serving a prison sentence for having sexually abused the children. Sarah was perpetually angry with the man, blaming and criticizing him. As the children grew older, she was completely baffled when they still sought him out. It was clear to me that her vast anger was perhaps more harmful to the children than the sexual abuse had been. On deeper inspection, we could see that her anger was self-directed and based in guilt. "How could I have let it happen?" she asked herself again and again. And eventually, after years of asking herself if she was a bad mother—she had become a bad mother.

Another danger to the child of divorce, separation, or death of one of the parents is that the child is in danger of trying to step in to replace the missing partner. The child sees mom or dad suffer and begins to take on the role of partner instead of child. The child loses his right place in the family and a disorder occurs.

It is important to the well-being of the child that he not attempt to fill in for the missing partner. If a marriage dissolves for any reason, the remaining and active parent must take great care not to move a child into the role of partner. When a parent becomes emotionally, financially, or otherwise dependent upon a child, this is very confusing and both parent and child lose their place. It becomes a form of covert or emotional incest.

During difficult times, it's essential for us to form adult support systems to help us weather these bad times and not to turn to our child for comfort and support. This is not to say that in times of family crises, such as a sudden death or extended illness, that the children be kept from the grief or suffering of the parent. They, too, are suffering, and families can grieve together. Children can and should be allowed to help weather a crisis, but we need to keep the child in the place of a child. I've seen many constellations where a child carried mom or dad's suffering and thus suffered needlessly.

Things to Consider

Before you begin any of the exercises to follow, you may want to create a family map if your system has been like the ones above. Think of this like a family tree where one system comes after or below the second system. Make it very clear at which point two totally separate systems have met and joined. Be very clear about to whom the children belong. Following are several suggestions to those who are attempting to blend a family. Choose those that fit and actively practice the suggestions offered. These are not exercises so much as daily practices.

1. Regardless of circumstances, offer only respect and honor for the former husband or wife. Come to terms with your own part in the relationship. It is important to take a fully adult stance with the dissolution of your marriage. In your mind return often to the early years when you and the partner still loved, still played, and still saw each other in a loving life. Hold those memories, and let go of the reasons

the partnership failed. Accept your part in the dissolution. This is easier said than done, and we have many, many ways of holding on to why we were right. You can't win with this thinking. It only extends the suffering. It is always possible to honor the other partner if you try to see the deeper soul—and see them as burdened instead of bad.

2.   Encourage the child to have pictures or mementos of the other parent in their bedroom or on their wall. Allow them to honor and remember the other parent without interfering. By doing this, you are insuring that the waters of life flowing out of the crystal reservoir to the child will remain free and clear. Making sure the child has his full life force is more important than your anger—or your need to be right.

3.   Watch your mouth. Monitor your own subtle comments and attitudes toward the former partner so children do not feel the need to split loyalties between their birth parents. Reassure children that, "Your father (mother) and I found we could no longer be married. This is not your concern; we will deal with it together. He (she) remains your father (mother) forever and my debt to him (her) is great—he (she) gave me you!"

4.   When at all possible, do not obstruct the natural movements a child will make between mother and father. Allow this movement and give full permission for it as long as it does not injure the child or cause him or her to be unsafe. There is no need to compete with your former partner for the child's affection. Your child will love you both—that love is embedded in his or her soul map.

5.   When you marry a partner who has children, avoid using the word "step" and accept that you are only the new partner. It has been my experience that children will deal with the "step" relationship over

time, eventually introducing your partner as their stepparent. Leave this to them. I've even noticed that sometimes it suits them to just say, "These are my parents," because, for some reason, they don't want to have to explain. This does not mean that the new partner has no say in how the household runs or that the children shouldn't mind the rules. However, when serious issues come up, the natural parent should deal with them. Some of this will change according to how old the child is when the new partner entered his or her life. Older children resist interference from mom or dad's new partner more strongly.

6. Refrain from pushing siblings from two different family systems into blindly accepting one another as brother or sister. They are not. Allow both systems their autonomy. If children are older, you may even explain to them that two families have come together but nobody is replaced or displaced. Again, depending upon how things evolve, the children will take (or not take) the other children as siblings. Let the child decide. Many stepsiblings become very close when left to their own process. When forced—you are in for a long, hard road.

7. Recognize that the children have the right and the need to experience the loss of the intact family, and only in this way is it their business. Children will naturally experience grief from the change that comes with divorce or remarriage. It is a fearful transition that can only be made easier if they are not cut off from the other parent. Be sensitive in helping them to ease the loss and reassure them that the divorce was not their fault—that responsibility belongs to you and your former spouse.

8. Be careful not to form taboos on what can or can't be talked about in casual conversation. Let your new partner know that occasionally you will recall and tell about the pleasant times with the former partner

for the benefit of the children, and to give strength to the new system. Remind him or her that doing so does not threaten the new marriage, and that you have fully chosen to be in this new relationship. Likewise, never ever use a child to "check up on" the activities of the ex-partner. This is terribly confusing to a child and rocks his world. Mind your own business. Keep the child out of your jealousies or regrets.

9. When a child is born between the new partners, this child now holds a place in both systems and is full brother or sister to both sides. With the new child comes a new challenge. Essentially, a new system has been born, and you are now blending multiple family systems. It is very important to maintain the right order so that the existing children are free to take the new child into their own system. Refrain from using words like "half-sister" as if the sister were somehow incomplete.

10. During any time of transition, pay close and careful attention to the children.

11. Notice if normal patterns are altered or if extreme anger, sadness, or fears surface. Respond to these emotions without coming down on the child. Help them to navigate the emotional sea in which they are swimming. Make all efforts to discern what is systemic, what is caused by the divorce, or what other issues may be going on with the child.

12. If your child has a different biological father or mother than the one he or she is being raised by, let the child know. This is especially significant if the new partner has raised the child since birth or early childhood. A sentence for this might be, "You are a child of my heart, but not a child of my body." We believe that even the soul of a very young child recognizes when something isn't quite right, and this should be made visible so the soul can relax. Be

honest with them when they are at a good age to hear it so there is no confusion. I deal later with the issue of adoption. Turn to that topic if you are adopted or have adopted a child.

13. If there is a question of paternity, address it directly with a paternity test and don't allow the uncertainty to fester. These secrets and questions can be painful to look at, but in the long run allow a system to grow in a healthy way. Some of the most disturbed clients I've worked with were somehow lied to on this most critical issue. The soul knows. In the rare instances that a mother is not sure who the father is, have a DNA test done rather than let it remain in doubt. The pain of discovery will be much less than the extended confusion that a child's soul can experience.

Adoption

Adoption and foster families present a unique systemic situation. The child, innocent and unaware, has been physically separated from both biological lines of his or her ancestry. Attempts to reconnect with parents or relatives can cover the full range of possibilities from sweet reunion to major warfare between the adoptive and biological families that may cause further damage to the systems involved. Or in the worst cases, the child seeking his or her biological family faces only rejection. Hellinger stresses that adoption should be a last resort only, and even then, a great effort should be put forth to place the child with natural relatives.

My husband, Milt, was adopted. His mother was Cheyenne River Sioux, his father was half Cherokee, and he was placed for adoption with a white university professor and his wife. His adoptive parents were kind and generous, and he was surrounded by the arts and an intellectually stimulating environment. In spite of these advantages, Milt spent most of his adult life working as an audio/visual producer advancing the many issues of Indians in our nation. He knew he was of Indian heritage, but was estranged from his culture and his family. When he finally sought out his biological relatives, he found two sisters and two brothers that he didn't know he had. It added another dimension to his life.

We cannot erase our link to our family system. Adoption is a painful issue for most adoptees. I have worked with dozens of adoptees and in almost every one there has been a gnawing sense of incompleteness. When I read Milt's adoption records, I discovered that he'd been left in the hospital or the mission for three months until his mother could be found to sign the release papers. During this time, the nurses and nuns who cared for him named him—changing his name from Dan to Charles to Tony as he changed locations.

We cannot underestimate the effect of this abandonment on the soul of that infant. It is biological, neurological, psychological, and spiritual. To complicate matters, Milt also fathered a daughter who was given up for adoption (unknown to him), and then later he adopted three Indian children—a systemic tangle.

As I mentioned in the introduction, within three weeks of being introduced to the constellation work, Milt found his missing daughter and has since formed a wonderful relationship with her and her three children (his grandchildren). He has also given full permission to his three adopted children to seek their families or origin.

Adoption also has an effect on the adoptive parents. This gets to be a tricky subject when I am teaching workshops. I always tread carefully. On the surface, adoptive parents often feel somewhat noble, as if they have rescued the child from abandonment. In our current society there has been a huge increase in adopting children from other nations and bringing them to America to *rescue* them from poverty and war. Two of the saddest constellations I've seen were with people who had been adopted and sent to a new country. There was such a tremendous longing to *belong*.

Society smiles on adoption and, on the one hand, the child has been taken in and given a home, most often loved deeply—and still there are those pesky hidden orders of love. In the midst of this good life and good love, the child still longs for the biological parents. They long to see a parent or sibling who looks like them, who has the same ears, mouth, color of hair, etc.

Here I again tread gently. Beneath the surface of social acceptability adoptive parents often feel deep within the soul a sense of guilt about taking another person's child. This can have many repercussions in how they act toward the child. Added to this, the natural, biological bond is not present, and the adoptive parent may feel guilty about that as well.

However, it's better not to make too many generalizations here—it is a minefield and I risk getting blown up. In my experience, the constellations of adopted people unfold in so many different ways that we simply cannot predict what will be seen. Naturally, the constellation may ease these movements, but there are still many inner movements that the adopted person might do to restore inner peace. First is the need to move toward fully accepting that, for reasons beyond your knowledge, your parents placed you in the care of others. Second is to recognize that despite the adoption, you are forever connected to the two ancestral lines of both your biological mother and father. This cannot be undone. It belongs to you even if you lack basic information about your lineage. My experience has been that adoptive parents who consciously "hold the place" of the biological parents will have a stronger bond with their adoptive child.

During one of Heinz's constellations, I had the opportunity to represent a young boy whose mother had given him up for adoption. It was an "open" adoption so the mother still had regular contact with the boy. I've never had a more powerful experience in a constellation than when I represented this boy. The pain took my breath away, and I burst into tears—I wanted my mom that bad.

If you have adopted a child, you are their caregiver—not their parent. If you accept this, it will ease your soul—and the child's soul. It is good to acknowledge that you can never replace the ancestral bond of the natural mother and father, but that you have been given the pleasure of the child's company and the care of that child for a short time. Acknowledge the source of the child's life in a hundred different ways. Be honest; be honoring. If the child comes to a stage of life where they seek the natural parents, allow it and stand by them if it is a difficult search with questionable end results.

If you have been adopted, you may want to practice some of the exercises below. Also, realize that deep down in the soul, where it counts, you can love both sets of parents. This love will have a different quality between adoptive and natural parents, but it is still love. There is no conflict. As an adopted person, you have suffered a unique fate, but it is fate. You did nothing to cause it. The greater forces of life itself determined this and you are innocent.

Things to Consider

If you have adopted a child that is not a blood relative, you may want to create a small alter or space on a shelf in your house and place two small plants, candles or something to represent the biological parents of your child. Periodically stand before these small representations of the people who have given so much to you, and thank them for allowing you to care for their child and raise him or her to adulthood. Tell them that you present no obstacle if some day they would wish to have contact with them.

If your child is inquiring about their biological parents, be willing to let him or her seek information about the parents. Stand firmly beside the child if he seeks this information and try not to cause any guilt. It is the child's right to know.

Exercise 1
Healing Sentences for the Adopted Child

1. "It was my fate to be placed and raised by others. I acknowledge and accept the weight of this in my own life."

2. "Regardless of my circumstances, I am linked by blood to the ancestral lines of my mother and father. I take them as my parents, and take my place in the ancestral lines of my parents."

3. Make a small sacred space in the soul to honor the biological lineage. You may further this movement by making a small, ritual place, something simple (not an obsessive shrine) to your natural parents. This could be two pretty rocks on a shelf with perhaps two rocks behind each one to signify the lineage of grandparents and those behind them.

4. "I honor all those who took my well-being into their lives and supported my life this far. (Include adoptive parents, grandparents, and any significant people who have helped you bear your fate.)

5. When possible, seek family members from your family of origin, but recognize that you are only the child and have no control over the previous actions. You must accept their decision to meet you or not, and practice seeing them with adult eyes—as people who suffered—and not with the eyes of a needy and frightened child. Again, a constellation with a trained facilitator may assist this process.

Extended Illness, Substance Abuse, and Mental Illness

The goal of this handbook is to provide simple things to consider and exercises to help families weather the daily challenges of life. If there are severe circumstances in your family, these small exercises will not be of great help. With extended illness, substance abuse, mental illness, suicide, and other severe events, you should not attempt to work too deeply within the family without seeking the assistance of a trained professional.

My experience has been that there are, very often, severe disturbances in the hidden orders of love, but we must treat these cautiously and with great care. I have seen too many modern, new age approaches that seem to blame the individual for his or her illness or even car accidents. This is not right and can burden the person suffering such a fate—or their family—cruelly and unnecessarily.

Having said all that, I think it bears looking into. Hellinger, in these later years of his career, has done many workshops looking at such things as cancer, heart disease, diabetes, etc. Sometimes, the work is simply to help the person come to terms with the hand that fate or the great unknown has dealt him.

During one workshop I had a client who had just learned that she had diabetes. With care and respect, we set up the client with a representative for her diabetes. At one point during the constellation I asked the diabetes what she had to do with—or for—the woman. The representative looked lovingly at the client and said, "I represent the sweetness in life that she seeks."

In many of the constellations I've done or seen when we used a representative for an illness, a missing limb, or even death, we see that the representatives never have an evil or bad intention for the person they are attached to. I find this more than interesting, and I think we are just on the edge of using this tool to examine the deeper issues that may influence illness. Hellinger has often said that chronic back pain indicates the person does not feel supported by what is behind him. Or they do not honor the lineage from which they come.

Once, on one of our trips to collect material for the native music radio series, we were invited to visit one of the women we were interviewing. Marge, a Tlingit woman, invited us to her

142

house for supper. It was the same year that my mother had passed away (and the same year I was introduced to this work). After supper Marge donned her mother's button blanket and did a slow, honoring dance for us in her living room. I am still not sure what happened to me, but when Marge finished her dance, I burst into tears.

I felt silly, but the grief and the tears were bigger than I was, and I couldn't stop. Marge was very kind and comforted me—and I just cried harder. The next day I woke up in our hotel room and my back had gone into complete spasms. It was extremely painful. We were due to leave Alaska that day and so I crabbed my way across the airport and made it home. The spasms would not stop. For almost three weeks I tried all I knew and still the pain was incredible.

Finally, one night I was lying in bed, and I said to Milt, "I don't know why, but I just feel so sad." He gently reminded me that my mother had just passed away a few months earlier. As soon as he said it, I began crying again. I cried all night and finally cried myself to sleep. When I woke up that next morning, the pain was gone.

I believe that I was grieving my mother and the grief had frozen up in my lower back. It did not quit until grief once again thawed and became just love.

Often I tell clients that a great deal of anger, numbness, and depression is just frozen grief—and that frozen grief is just love. When we let it flow as love again, our suffering ends.

Social Trauma and the Family of Origin

All of our discussion so far has stayed fairly close to the family hearth. We need to spend a little time talking about the many blows that can come from the larger movements of the world. War, immigration, political upheaval, being forced into refugee camps—all of these huge global movements shake families at their core. Our world is rocking.

When Hellinger first began to look into the deeper movements of the family constellation, he was working in Germany after World War II. His primary concern was how to keep families connected when the disconnection was so horrific. He discovered many things about war, about victims and perpetrators, and about what violence can do to families. For instance, he discovered that a bond forms between a perpetrator and his victim. When we have seen this within the field of the constellation, it looks almost like a love bond. When we see this, it confuses the mind and we can only wonder what occurs on the larger spiritual plane. We know, even today, that many soldiers come home having left a small part of the soul with the war and its victims. They can never quite come home. Again, this is too complex of a topic for a simple handbook, but I recommend looking into Hellinger's books.

Another discovery that Hellinger made was that when these issues of grief and loss go unresolved, somewhere down the generational line the roles can flip and those who were victims become perpetrators. I had to spend a lot of time wondering about this idea, but when I look around our reservations and see the amount of domestic and horizontal violence perpetrated by the people on their own people, it bears looking into. Or when a child who has been badly abused grows up and becomes an abuser.

I remember when I was a young girl, I could not understand why people would do horrible things to one another, or why war existed. Now, as an adult, I still can't figure it out. I sometimes wonder how we can turn so much attention to war when these resources could be used to feed, clothe, and shelter the world's children and families.

I've spent a lifetime trying to understand this. I do not get war. I never will. And in a simple handbook designed to introduce you to the shifting dynamics of families, I can't go

144

into my many thoughts about war and belonging and how the two interact. For those of you who also contemplate a world gone crazy, please check my suggested reading list at the end of the book for some of my favorite books on the subject.

Chapter Seven
Taking Care of the Self

In this lengthy discussion about systems we cannot leave out the body, which is a system unto itself. Actually, the body is perhaps one of the most complex systems known to man: blood, bone, tissue, oxygen, water, brain, chemistry—all operating day after day outside of conscious thought. Like the orders operating within a family, we have a personal physiology, our own system, which can also go out of order. Often we want to look out at the family of origin when a simpler solution is right at hand.

When depression or anxiety or other out-of-control tendencies take over, we should start at the simplest level first. Think of the body and brain as an elaborate signal system more sophisticated than any computer program you can imagine. We even have our own scan disk if we pay attention to it. When basic needs of the body are ignored or set aside, we begin to go off physically and mentally. Without a basic level of wellness, we cannot sustain any of what has been talked about in this book so far.

One time a client called me in the morning and said she was jittery and anxious and thought she was having a panic attack. I asked her what she had had for breakfast. She said, "Two Cokes."

There is not a single prescription or vitamin pill—or even a constellation—that will act as a substitute for decent self-care. On the most mechanical level, the body and brain need fuel, exercise, water, and sleep in order to function at all.

From Signals to Symptoms

When I was in college I went through a rather prolonged period of depression that took me to a place I'd never been. I sometimes woke up crying hysterically or spent hours obsessing about a professor who had introduced me to Carl Jung and Alan Watts. I thought he was my savior. During that winter I spent weeks huddled in my room listening to Leonard Cohen and pretending I wasn't home if a friend came to the door. With some effort I managed to keep up my studies, but was tied by a pretty thin thread.

I've often looked back to that time to try to figure out what went wrong. If I were going through this dark night now, some doctor would prescribe Prozac or some antidepressant drug. I'm so thankful those options did not become available. What I recognize now is that I did have a brain chemical problem. I ate sporadically and not at all nutritiously. I drank large amounts of coffee and alcohol. I slept little and didn't realize the healing power of simple. There was nothing clinically wrong with me. I was in a loop of lousy self-care that was messing up my brain functions.

Although this dark time may have been related to a systemic entanglement, or to the glass ceiling I was pushing against as a college student, my most immediate need was to correct my personal care patterns.

Many of us in the human development field are deeply concerned at the rising rate of prescription drugs used to treat what amounts to basic issues of life and spiritual grown. Recently I read about a woman put on an antidepressant for nail biting. Two weeks into her drug therapy, she began to see bloody body parts hanging from the trees. When she tried to quit the drug, she became seriously depressed and suicidal. The drug had interfered with important brain processing, and it took months and a great deal of agony to withdraw her from the drug.

While we shouldn't pan these drugs completely—mental illness is a real thing—we need to scrutinize their use. They can be deadly. The expensive ads that you see on television are simply that—advertising.

The body is an elaborate signal system and it is our job to pay attention. When we ignore important signals, it is like thinking we can divert a major disaster on the news by simply turning off the television. The disaster has already happened. Or have you ever had the electrical system go out on a car—no lights, no gas gauge, and no oil light? It's amazing how insecure and in the dark we feel without this guidance system. We need keep the lights on in here, in this body.

Once during a constellation a woman came to the empty chair beside me and I began to interview her. She was "high." Her eyes were glazed, her head listed to one side, and her muscles were loose as string. I asked her to tell me what drugs she had been prescribed, and she looked at me and asked, "How did you know I was medicated?"

From my own research, there appears to be little evidence to support the "chemical imbalance in the brain" theory of mental illness. In truth, the brain is always chemically imbalanced, constantly adjusting to our food, physical conditions, thoughts, and emotions.

Begin naturally, whether with yourself or a child or someone you love, to look at all the other factors that affect brain chemistry: eating habits, water intake, amount of actual sleep versus the amount needed. Next, consider what systemic involvement may be affecting you or your child. Finally, look carefully into your own thoughts and behavioral patterns to see what you are doing with inner pictures, words, and feelings. A great teacher of mine was once asked "What is the source of mental illness?" He said simply "Bad mantras".

Things to Consider

The body reflects what the soul is doing. Begin to befriend your signals and symptoms and to learn to be a better listener. What are some of the reoccurring patterns of your life both emotional and physical? Where in your body do you experience these things? Below are a number of exercises to help you come into closer connection with your own body.

149

Exercise 1
The Total Body Scan

1. Stand in front of a mirror and look at yourself from the neck up. Begin with your face and notice skin color and tone, clarity of the eyes, and whether there are any shadows or baggy folds beneath them. Pale skin, dry skin, shadows, general skin tone, etc. will tell you whether you are sleeping enough, eating well enough, drinking enough water, etc.

2. Now stand so you can see your entire body. How do the shoulders look? Drop them and see how that feels. Do you look like a carrier of something heavy? How does your spine look? Straight and strong—or stooped and burdened? Is the trunk of your body fully supported by your legs and hips? Do your feet feel like they carry you in a good way? See and feel all there is about your body.

3. Next remove all clothing and see the body nude. Notice any and all judgments, beliefs, dislikes, or other thoughts and feelings that come up. If you cannot see your nude body with appreciation and even fondness, the chances are you still have work to do.

4. Now begin patting each body part firmly. Say hello to the arms, legs, torso, head, etc. Keep patting until you feel the tingling energy begin to come into that part of the body.

5. Finally, gently explain to the body that you will now take more responsibility to feed and water and care for this body and to discover all that it carries.

6. And then begin to do so.

Constellating Personal Tendencies

It is a common practice for facilitators of constellation work to set up unknown elements within the constellation such as fear or loneliness as a way to gain more information. Usually the added element is free to move and roam and is not placed by the client. This has been very effective for me as a facilitator and can often lead to solutions that could not have become visible with the chosen family representatives.

As I gained more experience in this work, I began combining my NLP (Neurolinguistic Programming) work with the constellation work by inviting people to set up personal tendencies or behaviors such as the part that is procrastinating, sad, angry, depressed, etc. At the time I was running a weekly group on Tuesday nights. Many of the people who attended came week after week to participate and many did their own constellations. I was satisfied that the entanglements had been resolved, but not satisfied that all were beginning to overcome personal tendencies.

On nights when I only had one constellation, I would end the evening by inviting participants to choose a personal tendency that they would like to change. The results were often very startling and effective. Sometimes the tendency would point directly back into the family of origin, and we would end up doing a full constellation. Other times the tendency was some underdeveloped part of the person caught in past events, and we could work with this to point a new direction toward healing.

In similar fashion, we have set up a person's health issues, such as diabetes, heart problems, cancer, etc. or emotional illness such as depression, ADHD, etc. As with the tendency work, the client would choose a representative for the illness or a symptom. Most often with tendencies or illness, I would have the client stand in the constellation as themselves unless it enlarged and became a full constellation. Below is a brief description of how patterns form and why this tendency work is effective.

Within our own brains are stored all the key events that relate to our ongoing development. For instance, stored in the brain may be the kindergarten kid who was teased for being chubby, the elementary school child who choked on her flute

151

solo, the seventeen-year-old self who got pregnant, etc. Stored also are the larger events such as a death in the family, divorce, or moving to a new town. In simple terms, we could call these developmental insults or accidents—events that caused our development to stop or delay. When we have too many developmental accidents, we can't seem to hold all that life offers, and an undeveloped part of our self remains behind.

NLP is very solution-oriented and presupposes several things up front. One presupposition is that all needed resources can be found within (or without) to repair the developmental gap. A second is that behind every behavior and thought there is a good intention for us. Even the most violent thoughts or the most painful symptoms hold some valuable and are an important signal. When we don't judge the feeling or behavior as *bad,* we can use it to show us how to heal that part of our history.

For example, Fred had done several constellations and felt released from what he carried for his family. However, several months down the road he was still struggling with some undefined fear that wanted to leap out and stop him from making a forward movement. In a piece of tendency work, Fred set up a constellation using only two representatives: one for himself and one for his fear. He constellated the two parts and at some early point in the constellation I asked the person representing fear, "How old do you feel? Take the first thought." The representative said, "Twelve." I brought in a representative to stand in for that part of Fred. What I now had before me was a visible representation of the adult Fred—and his twelve-year-old self.

When I asked what happened at that age, Fred said he was twelve when his mom and dad went through a nasty divorce and dad moved out. The moment of resolution in this small tendency piece was for Fred to clearly see his younger self, how afraid and without resources he was, but to stay his adult age while he did this. I invited Fred to go to the boy and reassure him, to tell that younger self that he (the adult Fred) will never abandon him. In this way, a resolution was brought about by two parts of the inner system of self. Using this simple process, people have been able to look further into their patterns of fear, procrastination, addictive behaviors, and many other unwanted tendencies and to heal the seed event behind that pattern.

When difficult things happen to us, our developmental progress gets hung up. It is as if that younger self is lingering in the past, waiting for something to happen. From my previous experience as a personal issues coach, I've seen that two things have to happen before we can progress. First we have to stay our right age, and then we have to turn back and pick up the younger, unfinished pieces of ourselves and bring them into the current age. It looks like psychological work, but I believe it is neurological, part of the wiring and firing patterns of the brain. Think of neural connectors like dominos lined up next to one another—touch one and they fall in a predictable pattern. If we want to change the pattern, we have to line the dominos up in a new way—and then touch the first one.

Working this way within the knowing field of the constellation is identical to the work I did in my office, but is more visible and can produce greater movement as a result. I've been astounded by some of the shifts people have made as a result of this work. I began calling it "tendency work" because we were setting up parts of ourselves that tend to procrastinate, overeat, sleep too much, or are afraid to take risks.

At a three-day workshop in Orange County, CA, I introduced tendency work to a group where many of the participants had done multiple constellations. The result was a powerful combination of constellation work and supportive strategy work on inner systems and patterns. Generally, those who had never done a constellation needed to look into the system of origin first, but others now needed to look into their own stored brain material to see what was stopping them from moving forward.

Patterns are just that—patterns. They fire off in our brains often without conscious permission or knowledge. For the most part, patterning is good—it keeps the day organized. We can remember how to put on our socks, fix breakfast, or drive a car. Occasionally, a pattern forms in early childhood that is no longer useful to the adult you. A near-drowning experience at three years old has little to do with a forty-year-old adult who wants to jump in a lake. We have to retrain the brain to think a little better.

Things to Consider

Almost universally, people hate the part of them that is stuck (or ill). And almost universally, when we do tendency work, we discover that the unwanted part (symptom or behavior) is trying to get our attention, to show us the way to correct the problem. When we despise or ignore this important part, we end up continuing the pattern.

Some of the most beautiful moments in my experience with constellation work were when a person discovered some sad, abandoned part of the self, and then lovingly took that part back in with the promise to take good care of it. Just as with the regular constellation work, we are able to step out of the blind seeing of a child, and see our pattern with adult eyes. Hellinger called the difference between these two ways of seeing, "blind love" and "enlightened love." The first is childish—the second is adult.

For many of us, it is not the catastrophic events that cause us difficulty in life but the small ones, the in-your-face patterns that stop us cold. Crisis and catastrophe often cause us to reach up and out of the pattern pool to be larger than we think we are, but we must pay close attention to the signals.

Exercise 1
NLP Meets Constellation

This is an all-purpose exercise that, if you are wise, you will do again and again until it becomes second nature to treat your own self with the kindness, gentleness, and respect that you deserve. The better we become at reading and caring for our own physical and emotional signals, the stronger we will become.

Emotional responses of fear, anger, etc. are signals from the inner self that something is not quite right. Although we often wish we could just dump these unhappy feelings, we need to pay attention. They are the messengers.

When some emotion or old behavior kicks up and makes you want to scream, try the steps outlined below to discover what the messenger is trying to tell you. In this way, stress becomes a servant and not the master of your life. This exercise is set up as a meditation but you may also use your constellation objects to set it up as a constellation. My suggestion is to repeat the steps around many early memories that hold pain or other potent emotions. Pay attention to how you receive inner information—what combination of words, images, and kinesthetic or feeling information comes to you? If you want to explore this approach more fully, it is covered extensively in my earlier book, *See Me Beautiful*.

1. Notice when feelings arise (sadness, anger, feeling young and inadequate, fearful etc.) The nice thing about inner patterns is that they reoccur and are very familiar to us when they come.

2. Ask yourself, "If this feeling had an age, how old would it be?" Take the first age that comes to mind.

3. Are there any events/memories attached to this age/feeling?

4. Remind yourself of your current age. To strengthen this state, remind yourself of all you have done—your achievements, strengths, and highest aspirations, and

155

then confirm the room you are in, the temperature of the room, the chair you are sitting on, etc. Hold these adult resource anchors firmly.

5. Now make a quick movie of the old memory and be sure to see the younger self at the age you attached to the feeling. If it is not a clear event, make one up. It's very helpful to make the screen small, perhaps the size of a postage stamp, and at some distance away from you if the memory has strong emotions attached to it. This will make it easier for you to stay adult.

6. Now, walk into the movie set at your current adult age and take care of the younger self. Make him or her laugh and feel safe if possible. If not, take him or her out of the scene and go to a friendly place. Tell him or her, "I will never leave you to deal with this alone again."

Too often when we have a part of us that is scared or without resources, we try to push and shove it away, chop it off, or somehow get rid of it. Sadly, we end up repeating the original history of abuse—and the little self is once again left to deal with life all alone. Essentially, we become our own abuser, doing to ourselves what was done originally. It was awful enough the first time without internalizing it as a pattern and continuing it into adult life.

By inviting the feeling and all that is attached to it to come forward in the mind, we have the rare opportunity to make a correction in our stored history. Something unfinished is now completed. I call this rewiring the brain. Life is not much fun when we are constantly shape-shifting between the adult and the child. We want to stay our right age and make use of all that time and experience has given us.

If you decide to try this technique for yourself, begin with small memories or mildly painful events first. When you have mastered the ability to stay your right age and remake the movies, then try a more traumatic memory. In each instant, your current emotional signals will lead you to the memory. For instance, if your boss uses a certain tone of voice and you instantly feel small, begin there with that pattern. Step back, take a breath, and ask, "How old am I and what is attached to this feeling?" Eventually the technique becomes part of your strategy bank and you can take care of unhappy emotions quickly and efficiently in just a moment without being reactive. Early recognition is important. Don't wait until you are hiding in a corner or sucking your thumb all alone in your bedroom.

I once read that public speaking is one of the most common fears we have. We'd rather jump fourteen trucks than get in front of a group of strangers and speak. This unreasonable fear can almost always be traced back to some fifth grade self who had to make a speech to the class. It's as if the fifth grader is locked into the brain, and then the brain does all it can to prevent us from having to go through that again. When you think of how the storage of a small, fearful event or pattern in the brain can stop you from going forward, it's amazing. You are unable to join certain groups, unable to get your next degree, and unable to promote your work.

There is nothing wrong with you! These patterns are simply inconvenient wiring in your gullible brain and the wiring can be changed.

Working with Health Issues

Illness and health issues are similar to personal tendencies. They emerge as signals to the personal (or family) system that something big is going on—and being ignored. There are many facilitators of constellation work, including Bert Hellinger, who have used this work extensively to discover what we can about physical illness.

In my experience, many health issues are disguised metaphors for what is missing or what is needed. The illness has no "ill intent" but, like the tendencies, has a friendly desire toward the person. This is important to note. In all of the tendency work and health constellations I have done or seen, there is always a pure and loving intention. That symptom, or seemingly destructive part, is trying to tell you something. If you are not in position to set it up in a constellation, at least use one of the exercises below to sincerely ask that part of you what it intends for you.

Just as Hellinger discovered that love is always trying to flow within the larger system of the family, so it is with our own internal systems. Even when it does not look loving, love is beneath it. Try to see the love.

A final note on this, I recommend a wonderful book by Larry LeShan called *Cancer as a Turning Point*. This remarkable man was an icebreaker in this holistic way of thinking about illness and, from extensive study, discovered a relationship between cancer and a missing "zest" for life.

Things to Consider

As with all things concerned with health, please do not substitute alternative ways of looking at things for good, solid health care. At the same time, recognize that even the field of medicine can often not go where fate or the soul have been. Some of the most powerful constellation work I've seen concerned people who were facing life and death issues and finally came into the sphere of acceptance for what fate has offered.

Exercise 1
Constellating Symptoms

Begin this process by choosing a symptom that is not too serious. You will want to become familiar with this kind of deep listening to the body, and a little practice before you tackle any big issues. If you have a serious health issue, you may want to find a qualified facilitator and do a constellation.

1. Identify the symptom and get in touch with it. You may even give it a name similar to the way you did in the previous exercise with parts of the self. "I want to understand the back pain and its purpose for me."

2. From your constellation objects, choose a representative for your daily self and one for the symptom.

3. Center yourself and keep in mind which object represents the symptom and which represents you. Now constellate them.

4. Be willing to see this symptom in the new light of the constellation you have set up. Just notice its position. Does it look connected—or cut off? Does anything come to mind related to the symptom such as a person, a past experience or specific situation? If anything comes to mind, choose a representative for it and move it into the constellation. Notice if anything changes.

5. When you have a sense of the original picture, try moving the daily self closer to the symptom—or further away. See what thoughts and feelings come to mind as you experiment.

6. Ask yourself what that symptom might need from you in order to find relief. You are seeking the needed resources to alleviate the symptom and give it comfort. If anything comes to mind, choose a representative for

159

any resource that comes to mind. This could be a person, a food, a therapy, a bed (for more rest), or whatever comes to mind. Occasionally you may find the symptom connected to an earlier family member or ancestor and if this happens, it may indicate that your health issue is connected to a systemic issue. Take your time and do this carefully. Pay attention to any surprising connections between the self and the symptom that may come up. With each resource you add, check the response of all of your "representatives".

7. Move your symptom, the self, and the resources around and see if you can find the place of greatest relief and comfort for the symptom. If you get a clear message in your mind about what this symptom may need, you would be wise to respond to the message.

Note: It is not my intention to minimize the serious health issues that we all face at different times in life. I do, however, feel if we learned to pay attention to small symptoms and signals earlier and with greater care, we may prevent them from becoming serious.

Life by Design

We are all shape shifters, constantly dropping decades of time and valuable experience to become some smaller version of ourselves. This is not the road to strength. Once we have become free of any entanglements or burdens we carried for our family or origin, we are now free to design the life we want. Taking care of old developmental glitches allows us to move from *reacting* to *acting* in our lives.

Everything I've talked about in this book so far is about clearing the field of obstacles, both in the family of origin and internally, so that you can gain the freedom to create the life you desire. Over and over again I see people obsessively doing constellation work or other therapy forms rather than taking that step into the unknown.

In his book, *Love's Hidden Symmetry*, Bert Hellinger said, "It's a guiding principle of this work that knowledge must be transformed into action as quickly as possible. As soon as I've gained enough knowledge to enable me to act, I must stop investigating and start acting. Trying to find out more only dissipates the energy I need for action and knowing becomes a substitute for doing."

Whether you are facing a blank page, like I do on a regular basis as a writer, starting college, dreaming about that business you want to create, or seeking your life partner, it is this driving need to create that lets you know you are alive. It is the zest, the success, the charged battery, the source of new life flowing in your veins.

Robert Fritz, author of *The Path of Least Resistance*, says we all have a dynamic urge, a creative desire so strong we can't help ourselves. We want to bring new things into our world. Creating is not just the territory of artists or writers—it belongs to us all.

It is also what we fear most. What if we choose the wrong thing, do it poorly, or fail at it? What if we never discover what our life purpose is, that thing that makes it all worthwhile? This fear is so deeply embedded that sometimes we would rather not risk anything than to take a risk and fail.

Creating, be it a book, a nice meal, a beautiful space, a song, an intelligent business plan, a new career, a wonderful relationship is proof positive that nothing can compare to the

161

energy that arises when we are fully engaged in our own creation.

Things to Consider

You don't have to be "creative" to create. You simply have to be willing to face the empty void and see something in its place. When you create a small vision in your mind, all kinds of magical supports begin to kick into place: synchronicity, the desire of the inner spirit, an increase in energy, the needed resources. . . .

Many of us panic when asked to consider who we want to be "when we grow up," but my experience tells me it is not a big mystery. Just as many of our negative patterns were seeded into our early development, so we can often find the seeds of creation lying dormant there as well. What is play to you? What did you love most as a child? Did you prefer solitary endeavors or are you a connector? Did you love the big physical movements of sports and bikes and such, or the smaller things of puzzles, books, embroidery? Did the great outdoors call to you, or did you prefer to be inside?

Personally, I'm a dreamer but have learned to think big and work small. I see whole worlds but must somehow translate that into direct action steps. Explore the creative. Once you have cleared a few patterns, dropped a few entanglements, look around and ask, "What do I have to contribute to the world?" And then act.

Exercise 1
Developing Your Creative Self

1. Take your journal or a piece of paper and write a list, or better yet a wild cluster, of all the many activities that have given you pleasure throughout life. Treat it like a brainstorming session and leave nothing out. Set that list aside and make the cluster described below.

2. Make a list, or a cluster of all that you are currently doing in life. Name everything that takes any real time, including work, family, church, social activities, groups, etc.

3. Now, with both lists, do a simple exercise. You can do it with a fingertip, or you can actually set up a tiny constellation using stones or sugar packets, but touch each item on your first list and notice your energy—ask a simple plus or minus question. Does this make me more (+) or does this make me less (-)?

4. Now separate the two—the pluses and minuses—and ask very simple questions like, "How can I have more of this?" and "How can I get rid of or have less of this?" Make three decisions concerning what you have learned and act on them within a day or two.

5. In your journal, write a scenario of your ideal life five years from now—or ten years from now. Write this in first person using "I" statements and present tense, "I am." Now let your pen go wild. Do not let money, time, or educational level be a determining factor. Write the life you see. "I am living in a beautiful cabin along a running creek. There are trees around, and down near the creek is a small writing studio. . . ."

The temptation was strong to continue writing my own scenario, but you have to create your own. I can't do it for you.

163

When I open any group, we always start with an introductory round. When you do as many groups as I do, the same opening questions can get dull, so one time I asked people to say what was the *wildest* thing they could imagine doing. The responses were startling—in considering the wildest thing, I perhaps heard something closest to the life they most want to design.

It isn't easy, but neither is staying where you don't want to be. I see so many squander their dynamic urge by only wanting stuff, or endlessly remodeling, or using their most valuable resources up in trying to decide what car or movie they want. This is your gold coin, the dynamic urge. Spend it wisely.

Chapter Eight
Using the Constellation
for Other Purposes

The previous topics have focused almost entirely on the family of origin and the inner self. Now we leave that territory to explore the use of the constellation in other areas of life. I have used, or seen the constellation used, to explore personal tendencies, to solve work or organizational issues, with serious health issues, and to try to understand complex world issues. Every one of these topics could be a separate book. Hellinger cautions us not to work too big, but one of the most powerful constellations I saw him set up was between the Israelis and Palestinians. We can't help ourselves, we want to understand.

We cannot fix the world with constellation. In fact, attempting to fix anything takes us out of simply "acknowledging what is" and into naming something as bad or wrong. So, with this in mind, I explore several topics below to suggest different uses of the constellation process.

Constellation in the Arts

Here is a fun example of ways to use the constellation tool. A couple of years ago I was working on a novel (writing fiction is my other great love) and during a demonstration in Hot Springs, South Dakota, I decided to use the friendly group to try something new. Using representatives, I set up the two main characters of my novel in a constellation. I told them nothing of the story itself. The novel, *One Drum*, is a visionary story that takes place in Lakota country. The main female character, Terra, appears mysteriously in the Badlands and is actually an emissary of Mother Earth. The main male character, John Forrest, is a sad widower with two young sons. His boys find the strange woman, and the story leads to a great love between John and Terra, and a complete renewal of Earth during a drum ceremony at the base of Bear Butte.

In the constellation, I chose representatives for Terra and John and set them up. The constellation was great. Knowing nothing about the story, Terra's representative spread her arms out as if to embrace the whole universe and reported "feeling like the moon." John's representative couldn't take his eyes off her. He reported that she was glowing and magnetic—and that he loved her tremendously. They were both straight on with my characters.

I am not sure what this experience means, but I think of how actors and writers could apply the constellation as a way of deepening their understanding of their characters. When we went to Germany to interview Hellinger, he talked about a group that was using constellation to set up the great archetypal myths of the world.

Things to Consider
If you are a writer, artist, actor or dancer—or if you have some creative project you are working on—consider using your constellation objects (or gather a group of friends together) as a way to deepen your characters or get to know more about your work.. You have done enough of these small constellations now to use the process in whatever way fits your creative project.

Exercise 1
You and Your Creative Part

Whether you are an artist or not you are a creative person. You will only gain strength if you come to know that creative part of yourself. Here is a fun exercise you can do either using your small tabletop object or using a written dialogue in your journal.

1. Choose a representative for your daily self and one for your creative self or your art. You may also choose an object to represent "the future."

2. Constellate both parts of yourself on the small knowing field of your table or floor, and then simply observe their position.

3. Notice any feelings, sensations, images, or even words in your head that occur. If you want to stretch this exercise, try moving the daily self closer to the creative self. Now try moving the daily self far away from the creative self and see what changes.

5. Finally, find the strongest arrangement for both. You may even bring in other representatives for what you might need to make that partnership stronger. Point them all toward the future and see how that feels.

6. This has no real therapeutic value other than people who are connected to the creative are generally happier, healthier, and more fulfilled.

Constellations for Organizations and Businesses

The hidden orders of love that exist within families are blood bonds and very powerful. However, we find that similar natural orders exist within all groups that gather. A business, a church, an organization, and even your circle of personal acquaintances have all become small systems similar to the family of origin. Using the constellation as a way to know your organization or business relationships can be a powerful tool.

The difference between a family and a social system is that in a family all the positions are fixed and unchanging unless a new system is formed. In businesses and organization, the positions are fluid and changing. People come and people go. However, these social systems do set up an order within their borders. Authority figures are parent-like, and coworkers are sibling-like. Even a kind of birth order can develop depending upon seniority. And like families, things can go out of order pretty easily.

While we were doing tendency work in the Tuesday group, several people used the constellation to set up a business or professional relationship with a boss or co-worker with whom they were having trouble. The results were revealing and usually allowed the person to see things in a new way and to make better choices.

Most groups have a top down hierarchy whether that order is set up according to seniority, training or education, or other factors. When something occurs within these systems to upset the established order, chaos can ensue. When change is introduced into a system, it must be managed based on these established orders for the change to be successful. I've worked with many organizations that failed to recognize this and botched things. Too often I've had the feeling of having just walked into a family squabble.

One of the drawbacks of using constellation work within an organization or company is that there are no representatives who are "clear" of the operating dynamics; they are all in the family. It is often best to do constellation work with one or two key members and a neutral group. You can also use your collection of representative objects.

One client worked as a nurse in a large hospital. She used our group to constellate the main departments of the hospital.

168

The constellation made it very clear who was *seeing* who. One department felt unseen by the administration, the administration felt unseen by the community etc. What was interesting about that constellation was that nobody realized until we were almost done that there was no representative for the patients. This was perhaps the most revealing piece of the whole constellation. Sometimes we forget who it is we are serving.

In another organizational constellation, a group of colleagues were having difficulty communicating with one another. In the discovery process, I learned that this group had a founding member although the organization now operated as a team. The founding father was now just a "team member", and the earlier order of the organization was interfering with the new order. To complicate matters, there were actually generations within the team operating much as the birth order arranges a sibling line. While not as determinate as a blood tie, it was strong. A new structure had been imposed over the old without proper recognition of the "grandfather" and the elder aunts and uncles.

Another business I worked with posed an interesting challenge because it actually was a family business. All the primary players were family members. One older brother had been running the business for a number of years but was experiencing difficulties in his life. A younger brother had been promoted to take his place, and this had thrown the system out of order.

For businesses and organizations, the constellation is just one of many possible tools, but it can sometimes get to the heart of the matter quickly. Large, organized groups often spend a great deal of money and time creating a vision statement, doing departmental assessments, hiring consultants, all in an attempt to solve problems erupting from deeply embedded systemic disturbances. These disturbances can sabotage the best efforts of very intelligent people.

Perhaps the most common error upper management can make is to bring in an outsider or displace a long term employee with one from a "lower" rank without carefully considering and even managing the transition. If done carefully, these times of transition can be negotiated so that the change is made in the right order. For instance, a younger member who is being

169

brought in to replace an older member should have an appropriate time to "learn from" the older one. This honors the long-time employee, makes the best use of his experience, and also eases the younger member into place without throwing the system into chaos.

Likewise, we could use this philosophical way of viewing the world to look at communities, cultures, governments, and even nations. I've done a lot of work in Indian country and sometimes have to shake my head. If you take deeply entangled families with lots of developmental insults, a shared history of displacement such as that of Pine Ridge or Leech Lake Reservations, then you keep the borders closed (keep the white man out), and add to that the glass ceiling I spoke about earlier—you end up with the kind of violence and corruption I often see on the reservations. It is a downward spiral that is almost impossible to halt until a new generation takes over. Thankfully, I see this fresh possibility in the Tribal College students I teach. The new generations are gaining strength and insight, and the dynamic urge is a strong force for good. They want to start businesses, make movies, write books, and generally bring a new way of being into place.

Hellinger was wise to caution us not to think too big with the constellation. It is easy to inflate its purpose and think we can solve national problems or deeply-embedded cultural issues. In truth, we can only find strength one by one by one. And that is within our realm to do. At the same time, we use whatever tools are available given the opportunity. . . I leave this here for you to ponder. Some are event attempting to do what they call "Global Constellation" to test the true power of this knowing field.

Things to Consider
Whenever you want a greater understanding about co-workers or an organization to which you belong, try using the tabletop constellation to see into the system to which you have chosen to belong. Attempt any of following using the small representative objects in your basket or gather a group together and do your own constellations.

170

1. Constellate yourself and your coworkers or focus specifically on any individual that you struggle with.

2. Constellate the business or organization and the people it serves.

3. Constellate the levels of management and workers.

4. Constellate different departments within an organization or business.

5. Use the constellation to help you see into any possible changes in the future direction of your business or organization.

Remember that you are always seeking the order that brings the most strength to the most people. And don't forget your customers or the people you serve.

Chapter Nine
The Greater Force

As I come close to the end of this handbook, I find there are many other things on my mind. I first began this book prior to 9/11. It sat for many years as I watched the world change from that unhappy day. There are many of us who have long worked toward healing, education, serving others, and dreaming a new world into being. From my many years of working with others, I can see that strength comes first from the family, the two portals from which life pours into us, and then from the greater forces that surround us.

If we are to understand this great web of connection that exists within the family, we must also acknowledge that it extends further yet and includes the greater unknown forces that some call God or Creator and even beyond, that which can't be known.

Looking for God in all the Wrong Places

One of my trainers had a theory that many in the New Age—the vast numbers of people seeking God—are really unfinished or entangled children seeking a parent. Initially, I resisted and resented his oversimplification of what I saw as one of the deeper soul needs of our modern society. However, the longer I work with the constellation tool, the more I tend to agree with him. With all due respect to the great spiritual leaders of the world, I'm not convinced we can fully grasp profound spiritual teachings until we have fully taken the very source of our lives—our parents and ancestral lineage.

A guru or great teacher cannot be a substitute for accepting this source of our lives. It violates some deep spiritual order when a person says, "My parents were despicable and gave me nothing," and then turns all of his or her devotion and attention to a spiritual path. When we despise the source of our lives, it's as if our fists are tightly clamped and cannot receive much of anything. Our palms must be open and receiving life from the parents first and the great teachers after.

Joseph Chilton Pearce in his fascinating book, The *Magical Child Matures*, describes this need to take the parent as a fundamental process of human bonding. He says in order to be strong in the world we must complete a series of successful bonds within a nest of matrixes. Matrix is derived from the word "mother."

This nest of bonded links include sperm to egg, egg to uterus, fetus to womb and so on until the moment of birth, when infant and mother bond. From there the nest of matrixes extends out to include (in some order) father, family, community, country, world, and finally, universe and the greater forces that could be called God or the Creator. Even here, there is a right order.

If we impose Pearce's model over the systemic model of Bert Hellinger, we can see that the matrixes are also systems. For example, a functioning womb is comprised of circulatory, excretory, and nourishment systems working together to support a developing fetus. A current family is a system to support a developing child, and the family of origin, siblings, parents, relatives and ancestors, support the healthy adult.

Recently I heard a radio interview of somebody talking about human development. I only caught a piece of it so I can't tell you who it was, but he said that human beings are essentially born as fetuses. Unlike most of the animal kingdom, they do not emerge as independent creatures but as fully dependent. This struck me. No wonder it is so easy for our development to go awry. Like Pearce, I believe that our physical development must be completed before we can enter the wider realms of spiritual development.

One day, out of curiosity, I played with small wooden figures on a table top to see where I would place a spiritual teacher, a guru, or even God if I were setting such up in a constellation. My fingers wanted the spiritual guides to be out front as if beckoning me on. It seemed essential for the parents and ancestors to be firmly behind me as I attempted to move forward. It appeared, from my little experiment, that we couldn't place the great teachers behind us. It is not their right place. That place belongs to the parents, grandparents, and

174

ancestors who support our forward movements from behind. We should strengthen the familial foundation first and then seek the greater forces freely.

Healing the Healers

Emerging into our current world are scores of self-proclaimed healers, people who sense they have come into this life to do something significant. They have both need and desire to become healers and teachers and to somehow support life on earth. I highly respect this desire and feel as though some significant historical change is on the horizon. However, I also sense that we must be strong and fully prepared if we are to take these roles. Many of these new healers come from damaged family systems, their matrixes mixed up like a spider who no longer knows how to build a web. I don't trust their motives.

I worked with a client once who had Native American roots and who felt powerfully connected to Mother Earth. He looked with disdain on the world at large. We did an interesting experiment. I had him set up himself, Mother Earth, Mainstream Society, and his own mother.

In the constellation, Mother Earth reported that she was just fine. Society, however, stood in her place trembling with fear and quaking in the knees. She was weak, frightened and confused. This made something visible that I hadn't seen so clearly before. So many of us look to save Mother Earth, and do so by turning our backs on the child we have created—our own society. In this instance I interrupted the constellation because it felt as though I was treading on hallowed ground and should not take such liberties. However, what was revealed was powerful and significant and the picture stays in my mind.

Perhaps the message is that those of us who feel the call to become healers need to look first at our own selves, families, cultures and communities (in that order) and work there. Forget God and Mother Earth and the Creator—they can take care of themselves. Like a child who begins to parent the parent, we are out of order when we presume to think we can help the greater forces of our existence build a better universe. As a result, we get too big and then must punish ourselves in some strange ways.

Nature's Plan for Us

This discussion may or may not apply to all that has unfolded on these pages but it comes to, and so I write it. I again think of the dozens and dozens of people I've met who have a powerful desire to become healers or to contribute something to the world in which they find themselves. I would like to address it directly.

A few years ago we were asked to do a small radio piece for "Unplug America Day." This was sponsored by the Indigenous Women's Network and was intended to encourage people to use less, want less, and to unplug electrically. Oddly, this project once again took us into Indian country to gather information. One of the places we visited was First Mesa in Hopi country in Arizona. Up on this beautiful mesa is a village where the Hopi people live much as they have for thousands of years. Naturally, there are also televisions and computers and trucks in the driveway, but in general, life requires less there.

We went to First Mesa to document an effort to place solar panels on the mesa to provide sustainable electricity for the elders and people there. It was a good project, but I left the mesa wondering why we can't all live in this simple, conservative way? Why do we gather so much stuff? How does it serve us? This conversation has been going on in my head for years now and finally surfaces again here. My husband laughs when I go into my "gypsy" phase and start asking for only a covered wagon or a tipi to shelter me.

Although we laugh, it isn't funny anymore. The signal lights on Planet Earth are blinking and humming. Global warming, the ozone layer—as much as I dislike fostering fear, we need to pay attention to the body of Mother Earth and to care for her. We cannot witness such disasters as the Tsunamis, and Katrina, or sit here on the prairie and notice the unnatural wind, the dry earth, the lack of snow and the rising heat and disregard the warning signals of Earth.

Constellation work has taught me to see everything as energy, whether visible or invisible, and just as there is a balance of give and take within families, so does the same balance operate with all energy systems, including the one that sustains all life.

When we gain release from our system with a constellation, what is given back to us is energy. When we work to get money to buy stuff and to feed the body this is simply an energy loop. In essence, what I read and see on television about high stress living translates to me as an energy crisis. I think human beings take too much, especially in America.

This applies both to the beautiful globe we live on, and the expectations of what we individually can use or do. We have only a limited amount of energy to spend each day depending upon what we have fed our bodies, or how many hours we have slept, or how much water we have drunk. It's a simple formula really, except we somehow think that we can create more energy simply by wishing it were so. This I would call magical thinking. It's childish and unrealistic and makes us unhappy.

The time for a change has come. We need to recognize that all we are and all we use is energy flowing and being consumed. Somehow we have been trained to be consumers rather than contributors. We can no longer gather our energies only to pump them into more useless and endless consuming of stuff. Each of you who feel this same inner urge to move to a new place may want to consider your true energy needs. What do you keep—and what do you clear out?

Relationships, cars, equipment, clothing, books and all manner of stuff keep us hooked into the consumer role. Everything I own requires a small amount of energy from me—from a garden rake to a kitchen knife. Is it what we desire?

Begin in your own home. What stuff do you hang on to? What hangs in your closet or packs your shelves that you never touch or need? What surrounds you? Are you squandering your precious energy on stuff? Question each item separately, "How do you serve me? Do you add to my energy—or take it away?" Stuff is stuck energy, like congested sinuses or jammed muscles. We can't move freely or breathe freely when our energy is locked up in the things we own. We can't lift off like that beautiful hot air balloon yearning for the higher skies if we are tethered to our stuff. And we strain the resources of the Earth herself when we take too much.

Recently somebody emailed me this prophetic quote from a Hopi Elder. I found it very powerful and, since it came to me on the Internet, I hope I don't infringe on anybody by including it here.

> To my fellow swimmers. There is a river flowing now very fast. It is so great and swift, that there are those who will be afraid. They will try to hold on to the shore, they are being torn apart and will suffer greatly. Know that the river has its destination. The elders say we must let go of the shore, push off into the middle of the river, keep our heads above the water. And I say see who is there with you and celebrate. At this time in history, we are to take nothing personally, least of all ourselves, for the moment that we do, our spiritual growth and journey come to a halt. The time of the lone wolf is over. Gather yourselves. Banish the word struggle from your attitude and vocabulary. All that we do now must be done in a sacred manner and in celebration. We are the ones we have been waiting for.
> ~~ Hopi Elder

Something new is trying to be born into the world, and it is the stuff of spirit and soul and not material goods. We cannot cling to the sides any longer. We cannot cling and trust at the same time. In Pearce's book, *Evolution's End*, he offers the intriguing proposition that the human brain is not just a processor but also a receiver. What evolution intends for us is the almost mystical ability to reach out beyond our own brain and bodies to larger and larger sources of information. Pearce calls these "soup sources". In other words, knowledge exists outside of us and we can bring it in with the properly developed brain and enough energy to sustain a high level of being.

I, for one, am totally intrigued by this possibility and entertain it daily. I recognize more and more that I can't obtain this elevated state and drag all my stuff with me.

179

The Bigger Picture

Hellinger encourages us not to use the constellation to set up systems that are too large. Occasionally, however, he has done so himself when it directly relates to the client's current issue. For instance, I saw a fascinating piece which involved the famine in Ireland and the resultant systemic disturbances that evolved from that event, and Hellinger has done many, many constellations involving the Holocaust. The conference on this work in Germany in May of 2001 was on "Ethnic Conflict."

So, while we are encouraged to not attempt too much with this work, we also take small tentative looks into the larger systems of countries, national events, and relationships between larger entities.

For those of us working in America, we see again and again how history exacts a price from the current generation. Immigration, the Indian holocaust, the wars, and our own historical foundation are part of what makes us American. We cannot simply ignore these but can, perhaps, begin to adopt simple stances that allow for the right order to be restored.

All of my life I've lived in or near Indian country. Milt and I spent ten years wandering in and out of many tribal lands in search of music and stories. It's a simple step for my mind to take to realize that the native people were *first* in this country and have somehow been pushed into second or even a lower place. This is a systemic disturbance that must affect us all in some way and perhaps even contributes to the growing infatuation white people have with all things Indian. Perhaps our souls long to restore what was disordered.

We could also do more to restore the immigrant ties that were lost to those of us of European descent. I remember reading a report that said that the genealogy sites on the Internet were some of the most widely-visited. It would appear that we already seek our deeper roots—a necessary move in restoring the genealogy of the soul.

So often my clients know little or nothing about their family's roots or the important events that somehow many generations later landed them in the new land. When did we come? Why did we come? Who did we leave behind? What rituals, stories, and beliefs, were also left behind?

When at all possible we can discover more about our own historical roots, even when they are scattered across many continents. We can honor those who suffered so that we could take our place in this new world. We could also honor America's original people, the many tribal peoples that numbered fifty million when the Europeans first came and now number only one million. In a sense, the Native American is like the husband's first wife who died in childbirth. They forever hold a sacred spot in our system because, through all they suffered, we now live.

Several years ago, I wrote a novel in which an older Native American man named Albert had written about a vision he had had as a young man. In the story, I just called it, *Albert's Manuscript*. A couple of years later I was thinking about that manuscript and wondered what, exactly, it was. I bought a cheap green Mead notebook and sat down and wrote the words, *Albert's Manuscript* and began writing. The story totally consumed me and I wrote almost nonstop for the next six days. It was the strangest experience—the story was flowing out of my fingertips with almost no input from me as the writer. When Albert was in his twenties, he was an angry and unhappy young man. One day he got drunk and fell off his horse and fell into a vision that changed the course of his life.

In the vision he meets First Man and First Woman and they instruct him. They tell him of The Wind of a Thousand Years, a mighty wind that had begun to blow all the people of earth into one another. It would scatter the people of earth like leaves across the planet. First man and First Woman told him that when the wind ceased, the people would rub the sand out of their eyes and would realize that they no longer knew to which clan they belonged. They gave him many instructions about how he should help the people of earth to manage the aftermath of this great storm.

Every word of that story came to me intact, like a set of instructions. First Man and First Woman spoke of the four stages of man on earth. First there were the Watchers, then the Walkers, then the Weepers, and finally the Weavers. Its primary message was that we should pay attention to the children born on the edge of this storm because they would be the new weavers of the world. I'd like to end this book with an excerpt

181

of that story and the message it contains. If any would like to read the whole story, I'll include a link for it in the back of the book.

Excerpt from *Albert's Manuscript*

After First Woman told me a small part of her story, she became very no-nonsense and marched through the instructions efficiently. She went back into the gray walled structure and came back holding a nested set of metal bowls. They were of a deep, bronze color with thin rims of colored enamel, four bowls in all.

"Pretty, aren't they?" She picked each one up and set them side by side on the slab of cottonwood. With a tiny cloth-ended mallet, she tapped each one and a beautiful sound rang out. "I am using these to illustrate this lesson for you. I told you earlier that this chamber of open potential in the brains of The Weavers was fragile, a container only that must be filled. Actually, the inner chamber of the brain depends upon this nest of containers. This first, the smallest, is the mother and her womb. This next size is father and family. The third is the community, meaning everything from a neighborhood to the larger human community. The fourth bowl is the natural world and its many attending realms and worlds." As she spoke of each bowl, she tapped its edge and when all four bowls were singing together, that single fine sound seemed to contain all the music and stories of all the people perfectly harmonized into one sound. "Do you hear it?"

I was transfixed by that rare sound and could only nod.

First Woman touched a fingertip on each bowl to still the sound. She laughed. "That sound will put you into meditation and prayer. In fact, that sound is mediation and prayer."

She rapped each edge again with the mallet and let the sound sing out across the turquoise pool. I listened, feeling strangely moved and emotional. I never wanted it to stop ringing. This time she let the sound die out naturally but, even after the ringing had stopped, I could still hear it in my ears.

"They are nested, Albert. This is so important to remember. Each container holds the next container." She reached a hand toward the ground and a pretty silver pitcher was in her hand. First Woman nested the bowls together again and poured the water into the center bowl. When it was filled it poured out into the next bowl, and when that was filled, it poured out into the next, and so on until the water flowed back out onto the earth itself. "Do you see, Albert? Life, or more precisely spirit, is such an overflowing thing that if we just let it flow naturally it will fill every container. It flows from one container to the next, from one generation to the next and on and on. It is unending, this flow. But the nest of bowls must be in order. Do you see?"

"Yes, I see."

"Good. There is an order here that must be followed."

"Yes."

"Very good." She pointed to the pitcher of water and put it in my hands. "This is the energy of life itself vibrating. It is creative; it fills and empties and contains us all. I have it in this pitcher but in truth, it cannot be contained by anything and yet is contained by everything. Do you understand.?"

I did understand, and nodded, feeling like a schoolboy sitting beside my pretty teacher with the pretty bowls. Later, this lesson would prove to be both the simplest lesson, and the most difficult. The energy that is life, mysterious, felt and yet not felt, seen and yet not seen. It is immeasurable.

"Albert, when you understand this natural order of things, it becomes easier to be a Watcher, easier to see when a person or an institution has gone out of order. And a child in order will become a Weaver, capable of using this special chamber in the brain in very different ways, but only with proper training. My instruction for training the young Weavers is quite simple really. The key is to understand that the Weavers weave; one idea into another, one thought into another, one bit of information with another, one person to another, one country to another. They are pattern makers. They do not learn by absorbing information like wads of cotton absorbing liquid, but by weaving, integrating one thing with another. Our job, then, is to feed finer and finer threads and more colors onto their loom so that they can weave the vision. We could call them spider children but Weaver sounds better, don't you think? Do you understand? We do not learn; we weave."

First Woman stopped talking, to give me time to do my own weaving. I'm not sure what I had expected. I waited for more information and there was no more. She had finished the lesson with four bowls, and the instruction to allow the Weavers to weave. I couldn't resist asking. "That's it? That is all we need in order to enter the new time of gathering?"

First Woman shook her head. "Oh, Albert, you have no idea how difficult this simple lesson will be—for them to weave the new fabric out of the old? The challenges will be great as the Wind of a Thousand Years dies out. Earth will look like the aftermath of a great storm, and the people will cling to their old identities like life rafts. They will form false camps of belonging, fearful of separating or standing alone. They will reject the Weavers in a hundred different ways, calling them names, challenging their ideas, excluding them. Only those firmly planted in their families, whose center bowl can overflow into the other bowls, will be able to proceed. Old institutions of health and education will collapse and we must pay careful attention to the families and the food supply. The only grace is that it is the right time, and more and more will weave their connections between this earthly realm and the other realms. Help will come from other places. But the challenge will be great. Come, walk to the waterfall with me, and then you must go."

First Woman took my hand and together we followed the footpath to the edge of the twin falls. Neither of us spoke for many minutes. We walked, both lost in our own thoughts of spider children and weavers and the new world. Once she paused and said, "Albert, remember this. The strongest thread on the Weaver's loom is always love. Only love."

I knew my time in this realm was nearly completed. We were standing at the foot of the waterfall and I saw large, fat goldfish the size of my hand in the clear stone plates that held the water. Panic rose in my throat, and in my middle. I didn't want to leave this place, was afraid to crawl back into that broken body in another time and place. First Woman saw my panic. "And Albert, fear is the sharpest blade that cuts the thread of the Weaver's loom. And trust is the only thing that can mend the break. Trust."

We stood a moment staring into the falling waters. "Now, it is time for you to cleanse yourself. Walk into the shallow pool beneath the falls and put your body beneath its spray."

I started to object.

"No, Albert. All will be well. You must never cling to your belonging when it is time to separate. Go now into the falls." She dropped my hand and then handed me the small set of bowls. "Hold these close to your chest while you cleanse."

The twin streams of water flowing over the ledge were no more than ten yards away but it was difficult to force my feet to walk those ten yards. I knew. I must have known. I wondered if it was possible that the tears I'd wept earlier had merged with the waters above and I would now be showering in my own tears.

I walked into the shallow waters and then plunged beneath the falls, clutching the bowls against my chest. An explosion of water crashed over my head and shoulders and in the next instant I was blinking my eyes open in the disgustingly dirty and broken body of the Albert who had slid from his horse. Oh god, it was the cruelest of all awakenings.

Jamie's recommended reading list

Constellation Work
Hellinger, Bert, Love's Hidden Symmetry
Stark, Heinz, Systemic Constellation Work as Art
van Kampenhout, Daan, Images of the Soul

Human Development
Bandler, Richard, *Using Your Brain . . . For a Change*
Fritz, Robert, *The Path of Least Resistance*
LeShan, Lawrence, *Cancer as a Turning Point*
LeShan, Lawrence, *The Psychology of War*
Pearce, Joseph Chilton, *The Magical Child Matures*
Pearce, Joseph Chilton, *Evolution's End*
Ratey, John, *User's Guide to the Brain*
Smilkstein, Rita, *We're Born to Learn*

About the Author

Patricia "Jamie" Lee, MA

Patricia Jamie Lee has taught thousands of individuals to view their lives in a new way with NLP, Family Constellation Work, coaching, and other modalities. She is the author of multiple books, short stories, and nonfiction works. Her themes always include engaging life in fresh new ways. Her first novel, *Washaka* was awarded The Ben Franklin Award for Best New Voice in Fiction and was also a finalist in the PEN USA for Children's Literature.

In 2009, Jamie and her husband, Milt Lee bought ten acres of land in northern Minnesota and began building a straw bale house. Jamie and Milt have produced over 80 documentaries for public radio and television including the award-winning series, *Oyate Ta Olowan—The Songs of the People*. You may wish to visit their websites to learn more about their various creative works.

No Ordinary Life (Jamie's blog) at www.jamieleeonline.com

The Bead People International Peace Project at www.thebeadpeople.org

Video Letters from Prison (a film documentary about fathers) at www.videolettersfromprison

The Oyate Series and other documentaries at www.oyate.com